BEFORE ISHI

The Life and Death of the Yahi

STEVE SCHOONOVER

STANSBURY
PUBLISHING
Chico, Ca.

Before Ishi
The Life and Death of the Yahi

Copyright © 2024 by Steve Schoonover
First Printing

ISBN 978-1-935807-73-5 paperback
ISBN 978-1-935807-74-2 ePub
Library of Congress Control Number: 2024932908

Stansbury Publishing
An imprint of Heidelberg Graphics
Chico, California

Cover art: "Black Rock" by Steve Schoonover
Photos and maps by Steve Schoonover

Contents

Acknowledgements

There are people to thank, most prominently my wife of far too few years, Laura Urseny, who shared countless miles hiking in trails and nights sleeping on the hard ground. I have to thank my son Nate, for being the inspiration for this search, and sticking with us in the back country as long as he could.

I'm also most grateful to my former editor at the *Enterprise-Record*, David Little, who did a kindly brutal edit of this book. We had a saying in the news business: There are writers who need editors and there are writers who want editors. I'm one of the later. David knew that and didn't pull any punches. The book is better for what he did.

Nancy Leek and Ron Womack also gave the book an edit, and though they were gentler than David, they also made the book better. Bill Anderson also deserves a nod, for publishing in his *Dogtown Territorial News* a number of these chapters in their early form, even though I've since realized some of them were full of errors.

And finally, thanks to those who weighed in with advice, tips, compliments and insults as I worked through the process. You all helped, though sometimes not in ways you intended.

Introduction

The author's wife Laura at Black Rock in Mill Creek Canyon.

Before the Myth

This is not a book about Ishi. This is a book about the Yahi. They were the tribe that spawned him, or kidnapped his mother from a neighboring tribe, or this, or that.

The details haven't mattered because it's all been about Ishi. The tribe has been relegated to a mere frame around whatever myth about Ishi is being promoted, or whatever fable is being created from thin air to profit from his name.

The Yahi's history happened before a lonely Indian came down out of the hills into Oroville. The Yahi's history happened before the anthropologists dubbed him Ishi. And once they had a celebrity Indian in their hands, everything that had happened before became of secondary importance.

The anthropologists and others cobbled together a history of the Yahi to further the myths of Ishi, with easily disproved assumptions and legends about the tribe accepted as fact, without challenge.

The Yahi were said to have terrorized a stretch of Northern California about 100 miles long for years. Except, they didn't.

They remained unseen for decades by the people that displaced them. Except that wasn't the case.

They were a Stone Age tribe when the final camp was discovered in 1908. Except they weren't.

And Ishi himself, when he staggered into Oroville in 1911 to give himself up, was starving. Except he wasn't.

This isn't a book I intended to write. I had read the books on Ishi by Theodora Kroeber and Robert Heizer back in the '60s when they first came out. For some reason I picked them up again in the '90s after my son was born.

That's when it occurred to me that I could show my son historical sites in Yahi Country, like my parents had done as we moved around the country every two years due to my dad's Navy career.

The plan began unraveling with our first sighting of Black Rock in Mill Creek Canyon, although I didn't realize it at the time.

In *Ishi, Last of His Tribe*, Theodora Kroeber described Black Rock as "three times the height of a man, smooth and shiny."

In fact, where it rises from Mill Creek it soars 500 feet or so, and it's not smooth at all, but rather a twisted and ragged mass of basalt.

Kroeber goes on to have Ishi climbing to the top of the rock and looking down to the Sacramento Valley to watch and listen to a train go by. Well, Black Rock's in the bottom of Mill Creek Canyon, and you can't see the Sacramento Valley from there. As the nearest rail line is more than 25 miles from Black Rock, he wasn't likely to hear a train from there either.

"She never saw it," I thought of Kroeber and Black Rock at the time, but that's as far as it went.

As I returned to the books, I began finding obvious errors. Kroeber's narratives didn't match the firsthand accounts of the participants printed in *Ishi the Last Yahi*, which she and Heizer

The surface of Black Rock in neither smooth nor shiny.

compiled. Being a newsman, I turned to old microfilms of newspapers from Tehama, Butte and Shasta counties, from the 1850s through the 1870s, to seek other sources of information. And that process further unwound the story as it had been written.

I noted many of the mistakes came from an unfamiliarity with the country. Not seeing Black Rock was a fatal flaw. My wife and I began returning to Yahi Country again and again, backpacking the ridge tops and canyon bottoms and the high meadows at every opportunity. We learned how the land changed with the seasons, and how those changes varied from one end of Yahi Country to the other. We even backpacked eight days from the Sacramento Valley floor to Childs Meadow to get an understanding of the Yahi's annual migration.

That country tried to kill us more than once. I began to wonder how the Yahi could have lived in such a harsh land for eons. But the written accounts only sketched in a generic Native Californian tribal lifestyle and assumed it applied to the Yahi before contact with European civilization. The books instead focused on the Yahi's destruction and the time after Ishi came down out of the hills.

Reconstructing the tribe's history prior to contact is difficult because there are no Yahi left to ask. The anthropologists' questioning of the one informant they had — Ishi — appears to me to have been haphazard. Undoubtedly that is because of translation difficulties, but there are so many questions that just didn't seem to get asked, which would have cleared up so many mysteries.

Applying the generic Indian lifestyle to the narrative just doesn't work for the Yahi. Their country is a place of two extremes, different from the homelands of most of the other tribes. The artifacts they left behind are also different. They don't include a clear shift that happened elsewhere in Northern California a few thousand years ago, when new technologies came in from tribes to the north. The Yahi seem to have followed a different path — or rather, stayed on the path they had been following forever.

The only way we can imagine how they lived starts with learning their land. We have to do some speculation about how things might have changed since they were here, but that isn't daunting. No one since the Yahi has been able to set down roots deep enough to substantially alter what is there. There has been some clear-cut logging on the ridgetops, but it's hard to get logs out of the canyons.

Our science can then fill in some of the gaps. We know a lot about fish migration and deer migration. The First Peoples have shared information on how native plants were used. There is research on how fire affects the landscape when it's done with purpose, as the Native Californians did.

Even then, the Yahi lifestyle is somewhat of a guess. And for the folks who make their living on history — the professional anthropologists, archaeologists and historians — guessing isn't how you build a reputation and a career. You build on what's been accepted, rather than tearing down the research of your predecessors and starting over. That's one reason the mistakes about the Yahi just keep being regurgitated over and over.

But I'm just an old retired newsman without a future career to worry about. I can let myself logically tie together the things we do know to come up with a broader picture. And I'm pretty sure what I've come up with here about the Yahi is more accurate than anything you might have read before.

If nothing else, perhaps this will start a conversation.

Chapter 1

The ruggedness of Yahi Country is startling from the air. This photo shows Iron Mountain at the left, and Deer Creek Canyon winding past on the right.

The Yahi Way

The hill country between the Sacramento Valley and Lassen Peak in Northern California is tortured, more stone than soil, more vertical than horizontal. It's a wedge of volcanic material, laid down by eruptions dating back millions of years.

Over the eons, streams carrying rain runoff and snowmelt carved paths through the massif surrounding Lassen Peak. At the base of the high mountains, they formed a string of long, narrow meadows. Below, the creeks gouged deep canyons that empty onto the valley floor and finally reach the Sacramento River.

The land along the streams provided little that would appeal to most people looking for a place to survive over time. The upper meadows, with an elevation of about 5,000 feet, are covered with snow for winter's half of the year. The canyons below don't get snow, but there the sun bakes away life during summer.

And yet, in this environment, two populations found a way to survive in concert with one another. One walked on four legs; one on two. Today, we call the four-legged ones the East Tehama Deer Herd. The two-legged ones we call the Yahi, the name for "the people" in the language of the people who figured out how to survive in that country for thousands of years.

No one else wanted this land. To the east were the Mountain Maidu in the Big Meadows along the North Fork of Feather River. Their homeland plains were massive and diverse, and the small Yahi meadows next door were puny and poor by comparison. To the west, the Wintun in the Sacramento Valley saw the streams issuing through steep gaps in the escarpment that edges the valley, and saw nothing of worth in what lay beyond.

And besides, the Yahi had a reputation for fiercely protecting what little they had. Their neighbors could see little to gain and much to lose in Yahi Country.

The Yahi lifestyle had once been common among Native Californians. Though much the state the state, herds of game animals migrated as dictated by the seasons. Places hospitable to the animals in the cool, wet winters, would not sustain them during the hot, dry summers. And in turn, the summer sanctuaries would become brutal in winter. So, the animals moved, and at one time, a tribe of people followed each herd through the seasonal cycle, year after year.

Most of the other California tribes abandoned that migration about 1,700 years ago, when new technologies drifted in from the tribes to the north that allowed a lifestyle in which acorns became a staple food. The people could settle into more stationary locations, moving just short distances when essentials like firewood became expended.

The changes didn't take hold with the Yahi, judging from the archaeological record. They still traveled with their herd. Perhaps that was because the Yahi's fearsome reputation kept word of the new developments out. Or perhaps the new way just wouldn't work in Yahi Country. Or perhaps after thousands of years of living intertwined with their herd, the Yahi just weren't interested in a change.

The relationship between the Yahi and their herd wasn't like what hunting is today. Rather than spending a few days seeking a kill, the Yahi spent the whole year with their deer. It was a full-time job that gave them a better knowledge of the animals among them, and what the herd needed to thrive. The Yahi used fire to improve the deer's food supply, as lush growth followed a burn in those days. There was killing of course, but not of the animals critical to the herd. The Yahi knew their survival depended on maintaining the health of the herd.

The cycle

Just before winter turned to spring, the people would be scattered at villages along the streams through the foothills. The canyons of Deer Creek, Mill Creek, Antelope Creek and a few others are steep, even sheer for most of their length. But there are places where the gorges open for a distance. The cliffs that elsewhere loom close over the waterways retreat a mile or two, creating basins of sorts. In these spots, relatively flat land can be found streamside, and the surrounding slopes are less abrupt. Plants and animals don't have to cling to cliffs to survive.

At this time of year in each of these basins, there would be a village composed of an extended Yahi family. There weren't many of them, perhaps a dozen families or so, with a total population for the tribe below a thousand.

Winter was most wrought with danger for the Yahi. The weather would have hindered their hunting, and there are few food plants that ripen in that season. They would be relying on food gathered and stored in fall, with the hope they had enough to make it through the cold times. They would have put up acorns, berries, pine nuts and other seeds. Deer, other animals and fish would have been harvested and dried to last until spring.

But in spring, the foothills awakened. The land produced a feast of edible plants, and flowers rose above the grass to mark the location of the bulbs beneath. Game came out of hiding, and the hunters were less restricted by weather.

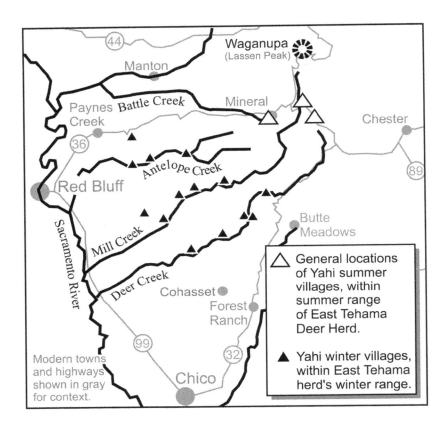

And more important, the streams turned silver with migrating salmon. With each heavy rain that sent a major flow of water downstream, a flow of spring-run chinook salmon would come up into the canyons.

We can only guess on the number of fish that came upstream, but they likely numbered into the tens of thousands. All worries vanished about whether the food supplies would last, because the earth had replenished the Yahi's stores. They would net and spear the fish, eat their fill and dry extra for use later.

As it was with the deer herd, they had a responsibility. They knew to not catch too many, so enough salmon could fill the deep, cool pools of the streams. The fish would spend the summer there and spawn and die in fall. After hatching, their fingerlings would move downstream and out into the ocean.

And the Yahi knew if they let that happen, those surges of fish would come up the Yahi streams next year at the hungry time, just when they were needed, and the next year, and the next, and the next, until the end of time.

But the seasons were changing. The foothills bake to barrenness early in the year. Gullies that had carried streams all winter go dry early in spring. The ridge top grasses bleach in the sun from green to pale gold — the color of summer. That dry color spreads quickly down into the basins. Life shrivels to narrow bands along the few streams that still flow.

However farther uphill, spring comes later and stays later. When the winter range parches, the land is still green just a few miles higher east. Snow-fed streams gush through banks of ferns, and wildflowers bloom, months later than their cousins below.[1]

It was what the deer needed in summer, so they moved from the canyons to the high meadows.[2] And the people came as well.

The Yahi migration upstream wasn't rushed. They would move from one site to another and settle in for a few days. Each place was one where they'd camped each year for decades, or even centuries. Each time the people had stopped there, plants that produce food in spring had been harvested and then cultivated so they would be ready to serve the people's needs again the next year.

The brodiaea provides an example. In spring the starchy bulb — sometimes called Indian potato — sends forth a

Brodiaea flowers. The blooms mark the location of an edible bulb.

cluster of blooms, usually blue or purple but sometimes white. It would tell the Yahi where to dig. And when they dug, around the base of the main bulb that was about the size of a golf ball, they would sometimes find smaller bulbs the size of a pea or smaller.

The large bulbs would be eaten. The small bulbs would be returned to the soil, spread over a larger area. And in a few springs, as the migration passed through again, some of the smaller bulbs would now be large enough to harvest, with their own crop of smaller bulbs for future migrations.

Caring for the crops was the women's job. The men would hunt and fish in the vicinity, until it was time to move again.

Over and over the Yahi would repeat the pattern of moving and resting, until each family reached a wishbone-shaped valley and string of high meadows that would be the summer home of all the people.

In winter they'd been scattered along a number of streams, isolated from one another by the ruggedness of their country. But all the streams along which they wintered flowed from the same area, so the migration upstream brought the people together. As the Deer Creek families moved upstream, they'd complete their migration on the eastern arm of the wishbone, near the place now known as Childs Meadow. The Mill Creek brethren would arrive at the same general area, coming up the western arm of the wishbone to a place that today is Morgan Valley. The two streams, several hours walk apart for most of their length, came within a half-mile of each other at this point.

From Antelope Creek, Paynes Creek and perhaps farther north, the people would end their migration in the grassy basin now called Battle Creek Meadows. This place is separated from the other Yahi meadows by only a few miles across one of two relatively mild gaps in the mountains.

It was here that the Yahi language probably formed, for only here was there ready contact between the families. The people could move back and forth through this country fairly easily. Although the area was higher, it was a gentler terrain than the deep canyons where winter was spent.

From each family's camp, smoke could be seen rising nearby from people who were distant for the rest of the year. Old friends from neighboring camps would seek out each other. News would pass from family to family. New mothers would show off babies to relatives they hadn't seen in a year. Boys who were turning to men would notice childhood playmates from other families were now turning into women.

A twisted shrub struggles to survive on a ridge in Yahi Country.

A successful hunt might not be a time for a feast by a single family, but rather a celebration for two families or more. Men might join together and leave for nearby campgrounds for hunts, or to make the risky trek east across Maidu country to the Warner Mountain obsidian quarries. Perhaps a joint trade expedition might be mounted across the mountains to the north, to the friendlier people along Hat Creek.

And so it would go for the summer. It was a happy time for the hunters. The meadows would stay green after all else had dried up, and therefore would be a magnet for life of all kinds. Deer would move down out of the hills at dusk to graze, almost invisible in the dimming light. Also invisible would be the hidden hunters awaiting them.

There would be feasting and dancing, boasting and joking, gambling and storytelling, courting and marrying between the families.

But the meadows are high in the mountains — around 5,000 feet — and after a few months, each band of clouds would bring snow rather than rain. Along the creeks, the leaves of the big leaf maple would turn golden and flutter downward with each gust of wind, like giant butterflies allowed just a single flight.

It would be time to move again.

With a circuit of final feasts, the families would say goodbye for another year, and scatter back toward their winter camps.

The downhill migration likely went quicker, as the abundance of spring would be missing from the stops along the way. The people would hurry down to the streamside pockets where the families would pass the winter, for there was work to do.

Old houses would be repaired; new houses would be built. As they had in the spring, the people would scatter to nearby sites to harvest food. Acorns would be gathered from the blue oaks and live oaks in the canyons, or from the black oaks up on the ridgetops. Berries would be picked and dried, seeds gathered and stored.

It was the easiest season for hunting deer. It was rutting season, and the bucks lost any sense of caution. In addition, the rains would not yet have returned abundant water to the foothills. The herds would have to concentrate around the limited water sources, where the men would hunt them vigorously. Animal after animal would be brought down into the camps. The people would eat the fresh meat heartily, and dry vast amounts to carry them through winter. The skins would be cured to provide cover from the coming cold.

It is possible that the Yahi moved to the Sacramento Valley floor to fish for the salmon that ran upstream in fall. Unlike the salmon runs in spring, the fall runs spawn on the flatlands rather than in the canyons, and there's ethnographic data that suggests the Yahi had agreements with the valley tribes that allowed them access to this resource.

Women prepared basketry materials. Men stored obsidian, basalt and other materials needed for making bows and arrows.

It also was the beginning of the time for fire. California was made to burn. Any place where the rains all but stop for five or six months of the year is going to burn. What the First Peoples did was learn to control what burned. They didn't wait for lightning to ignite a dry grassy range, or a ravine choked with brush. Instead, in the wet seasons they lit off the places where fire's benefit hadn't been felt in a while. That kept the landscape from becoming overgrown and laden with the dead wood that modern firefighters call fuel.

In the native way, when lightning did strike, the blazes it caused were calm and sedate, rather than the raging infernos that today climb into the crowns of trees and race through our modern forests.

Throughout California in those days, fire wasn't a destructive force but rather awakened the land. The native plants had evolved to thrive in that condition. Lush greenery followed a burn. Many shrubs grow quickly from the crown of their roots after a burn. Some seeds require fire to sprout. Most of the common dry land trees have fire-resistant bark to survive the flames.

As the days went by, morning chill would turn to morning frost. Light rains would become more strident and colder. The country would turn hostile, and the people would retreat to their homes, and await spring.

The cycle would continue as it had for thousands of years. But it wasn't destined to continue forever.

NOTES

1. My wife Laura and I had a graphic experience with elevation's effect on the seasons in late May/early June of 1995, when we backpacked from the Sacramento Valley floor to Childs Meadow to experience something similar to the Yahi annual migration. The first day, from the bottom of the Hogsback southeast of Red Bluff to Antelope Creek — elevation 400 to 900 feet — the temperature topped 100 degrees. Six days later, walking into the village of Mill Creek -- elevation 4,700 feet -- we were snowed on.

2. There is an alternative theory about the migration of the East Tehama Deer Herd — with which I do not agree — that most of the deer migrated to the Sacramento River in the spring. The author of the theory reasoned that before white men introduced logging, there would have been a dense band of forest between the foothills and the high meadows with little food for deer. I think the author formed an incorrect idea of what Yahi Country would have looked like before logging. He also ignored the historical accounts of the Forty-Niners who came to California on the Lassen Trail, right through Yahi Country. They reported large numbers of deer in the vicinity of high meadows as they passed through in fall, right where they can be found today at that time of year.

Chapter 2

The high meadows below Lassen Peak were the Yahi heartland, where the tribe came together for part of the year and where their shared language may have formed.

One split too many

When anthropologists began trying to reconstruct native California, after it had been ravished almost beyond recognition, they brought some preconceptions to the table. They sought to break Native California into the kinds of nation states that existed in the rest of the world, and even in other Indian cultures in America.

It was a mistake, as California Indians really didn't organize into nations or the larger tribes found farther east. Instead they were a series of separate villages, making their own choices, independent of one another.

Still they were grouped, based on languages common to the various villages. Here was the Maidu nation; there the Wintun. And there in the southern Cascade Mountain foothills were the Yana.

Almost immediately, it was recognized the picture had been painted with a brush too broad, and the larger groups were broken apart. The Maidu became the Nisenan, the Konkow and the Mountain Maidu; the Wintun became the Wintu, Nomlacki and Patwin.

The Yana were split too, first into two groups, then three and finally four.

That is, I believe, one split too many.

In 1874, Stephen Powers in his *Tribes of California* split the Yana into the Nozi in the north, and the Kombo in the south. The territory was later redivided into the Northern, Central and Southern Yana.

In 1911, a survivor from one of the Yana bands came into civilization in Oroville. Given the name Ishi by the anthropologists who took him in for the final five years of his life, he was identified as a Yahi, a previously unknown group. With that, Yana country was divided yet again, with the canyons of Deer and Mill creeks — which Ishi called home — being severed from Southern Yana lands.

It was thought the difficulty in moving north to south allowed four separate dialects to form. Yana country is a succession of east-west canyons. The people in each canyon might have contact with those over the ridge to the north and over the ridge to the south, but not much beyond that. Over the full distance from north to south, the division into four distinct tongues seems plausible.

But the idea breaks down in Yahi country. If the Yana language was going to fragment because of the difficulty of moving from north to south, why didn't it crack along the most substantial barrier between two canyons in the entirety of that Yana/Yahi country -- namely the ridge between Deer Creek and Mill Creek?

Those two canyons are the deepest and most rugged in the whole of that country. Crossing between them is a major task, even today, even with modern motorized vehicles. If the Yana

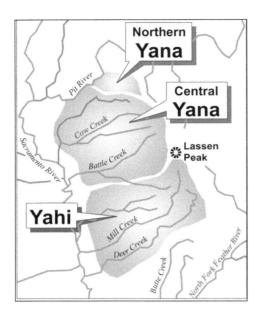

language was going to fracture, this was an obvious place.

Moving from one canyon to another would have been so time-consuming and difficult that it only would have been undertaken for special purposes. Contact between the canyons could not have been a regular thing, or something critical to the survival of the people. It would not have required a common language, just enough shared words to avoid conflict and make trades. So why would they have a common tongue?

The answer lies in the summer range. Mill Creek and Deer Creek rise in the same area, and people moving upstream for summer along either stream would have ended up in the same neighborhood. As the separate Yahi groups came together for the summer, development of a common language seems very plausible.

When I first started studying the Yahi, I developed what I think is a common misconception: That the canyons are the Yahi heartland, and the trip to the summer meadows was a seasonal excursion, almost a vacation. I now believe that's backward. I think the Yahi regarded the high meadows as their heartland, as that was where they got the closest to being a single people. The canyons were places the Yahi were forced into by winter, which was a time of isolation and hardship.

The same reasoning works for the Central Yana dialect. Head up any of the streams in that country and you end up in the same general neighborhood. Conveniently, there is a deer herd — now called the Cow Creek Herd — which occupies the same general area as the Central Yana, and follows a migration pattern similar to the East Tehama Herd. The animals winter low in the foothills and climb in summer to higher meadows. It seems logical that the Central Yana followed that herd, and that people's dialect shaped in the meadows where they gathered in summer.

The Northern Yana occupied a much smaller area, and weren't believed to have followed the same seasonal migration, although that band's two main streams both come together as you move upstream.

Only for the Southern Yana does the pattern break down. Their territory, according to the anthropologists, was centered on Battle Creek. As you move up Battle Creek's two main forks, they spread wide. Indians following the South Fork would end up in Battle Creek Meadows near the Yahi summer grounds; those following the North Fork would end up with the Central Yana.

However there may not have been a Southern Yana dialect distinct from the Yahi.

Linguists know little of the Southern Yana language. Those people were believed to be extinct when information gathering began, and few of their words are known. But the few words of Southern Yana that are known are identical to their Yahi counterparts.[1]

The Northern Yana and Central Yana dialects are closely related, and there's a significant difference between them and their neighbors or neighbor to the south.

There is a suffix "-hee" applied to some masculine nouns in Southern Yana and Yahi, that is missing in the Northern and Central dialects. It its place they use only the suffix "-nah," which also occurs in some Yahi and Southern Yana terms. The two suffixes serve generally the same purpose as the words "a" "an" or "the" in English, if I understand the linguists correctly.

The most obvious examples of the difference are in the words used to identify the people who spoke them. In the north and center, "the people" would be "Yah-nah" or Yana; in the south they would be "Yah-hee," or Yahi.

Thus, Southern Yana men would have called themselves Yahi. The anthropologists, not knowing that, probably assumed they had found a fourth and previously unknown group when the Northern Yana Sam Batwi — brought in to translate for Ishi

— associated him with the Yahi.

But if that's the case, to which group would the Yana along Battle Creek have belonged?

In Alfred Kroeber's *Handbook of the Indians of California*, he says the Northern Yana called their dialect Gari'i and the Central called theirs Gata'i. Writing about Southern Yana as distinct from Yahi, he continues: "The southern dialect is extinct: it may have been included in Gata'i."

What he's saying is the Indians along Battle Creek may have been Central Yana.

Further, Ishi had a single word — Gari'si — for the Yana who were not Yahi, and that included those Indians who lived along Battle Creek. Another word, Ga'me'si, he applied to Yahi country, and that may be a Yahi name for the dialect spoken there. Both these clues suggest Battle Creek — at least its lower stretches and North Fork — was Central Yana territory.

If this model is correct — if the dialects formed in the summer ranges — everything from the Paynes Creek watershed south to Deer Creek would have been Yahi country. As you head upstream along all the waterways in that stretch, you move towards the Yahi summer range.

Battle Creek and the streams north of that would have been Yana. Again, the streams all flow from the same general area.

We have to remember that these groupings are linguistic, not political. There was no larger, all-encompassing structure. It makes for an untidy map, but there's really no reason to divide Yana territory into three or four or five sharp divisions. Our linguistic groupings may all be artificial.

But, they are useful; useful enough that we continue to use them.

NOTE

1. For much of this I am grateful to the late linguist Victor Golla, with whom I communicated in the 1990s. Those contacts contributed to this theory back in that decade. In Golla's 2011 book *California Indian Languages,* he divides Yana into three dialects: Northern, Central and Southern, with Yahi a subdialect of Southern Yana.

Chapter 3

Lower Deer Creek Falls provides a clue to where a number of villages Ishi drew on a map correspond to the terrain of Yahi Country.

Placing Ishi's villages

After the man who came to be known as Ishi came out of the hills in 1911, he created a map centered on the country along Mill and Deer creeks, the canyons into which the Yahi had retreated by the time he was born.

The map is included in Alfred Kroeber's 1925 publication *Handbook of the Indians of California*.

Ishi marked out five villages along Deer Creek in Yahi territory, two on Mill Creek and one between the two streams.

However there are hundreds of archaeological sites along the two streams. Trying to pick eight sites that might be those Ishi mapped is a fool's errand.

However if you can step away from a mental bias of Western civilization, Ishi's map actually corresponds quite closely to the terrain along the two creeks.

Today we look at our communities as specific places, albeit with a changing cast of characters. Everyone can find Chico or Red Bluff on a map. Everyone knows where San Francisco and New York are.

However if you think of a community as its people rather than where they are located, Ishi's map becomes a description of their locations relative to each other.

With that change of perspective, his map matches quite nicely with the creekside pockets in the Yahi winter range where the families sought shelter, and the meadows higher up the creeks in the summer range where they all came together as a tribe.

The idea that Ishi was mapping people rather than locations corresponds with something Kroeber wrote in his chapter on the Yana and Yahi, in which the map appears.

"Tuliyani on Mill Creek and Yisch'inna on Deer Creek, may be the names of chiefs that once lived at those villages rather than true place names," Kroeber wrote.

There are a couple of clues in Ishi's map that allow us to speculate about the names of general areas where the Yahi villages were located in winter and summer.

The prime clue is his mapping of a lake — Hatichamauna — south of Deer Creek.

There is no lake in that direction from Deer Creek anywhere along its length. However there is a lake — now called Wilson Lake — that could match Ishi's map, and it is in the neighborhood of the high meadows.

Wilson Lake is east of Gurnsey Creek, rather than south of Deer Creek, but it has the same geographic relationship to Deer Creek as shown on Ishi's map. Wilson Lake is to the right of the stream when heading upstream, just as it is on Ishi's map.

Deer Creek splits in Deer Creek Meadows. The larger of the two streams heads north — becoming Gurnsey Creek — and it's easy to assume the Yahi regarded it as Deer Creek's main stream. Gurnsey Creek also rises close to Mill Creek on the way to Lassen Peak, just as Deer Creek does in Ishi's map.

If this theory is correct, it would put the village Ishi called

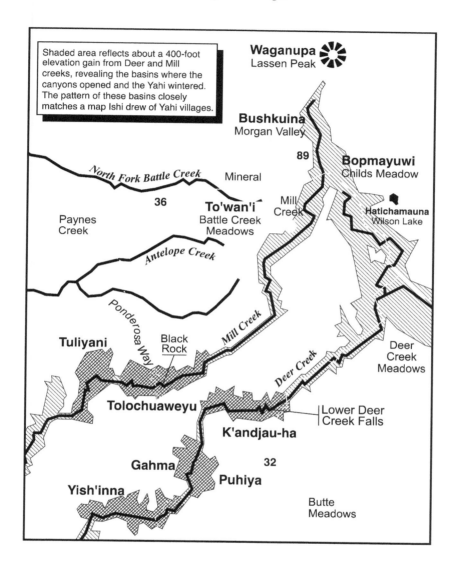

Shaded area reflects about a 400-foot elevation gain from Deer and Mill creeks, revealing the basins where the canyons opened and the Yahi wintered. The pattern of these basins closely matches a map Ishi drew of Yahi villages.

Waganupa
Lassen Peak

Bushkuina
Morgan Valley

89

Bopmayuwi
Childs Meadow

North Fork Battle Creek   Mineral

36   **To'wan'i**
Paynes   Battle Creek   Mill
Creek   Meadows   Creek

Hatichamauna
Wilson Lake

Antelope Creek

Ponderosa Way

Tuliyani   Black
Rock

Mill Creek

Deer Creek

Deer
Creek
Meadows

Tolochuaweyu

Lower Deer
Creek Falls

K'andjau-ha

Gahma   32
Puhiya

Yish'inna

Butte
Meadows

Bopwayuwi in Childs Meadow. Bushkuina would be in the meadows along Mill Creek, an area known as Morgan Valley.

That leaves two villages on Mill Creek and four on Deer Creek in the Yahi winter range, down the canyons. These probably correspond to the basins there — those places where the canyon tops ease back from the creek, creating small pockets of relatively flat land.

Wilson Lake; known perhaps as Hatichamauna to the Yahi.

Of the canyon villages, Ishi designated three as "rich." Two are the villages on Mill Creek; one is on Deer Creek.

Conveniently this pattern matches the three largest basins along the creeks, which could be expected to have more resources, support a larger population and be "richer" than the others. On Mill Creek, one basin lies between Long Point and Table Mountain, and the other is upstream from Long Point, in the vicinity of Black Rock. The rich Deer Creek basin is in the area of Iron Mountain.

Ishi indicated a trail ran from the rich Deer Creek village, Yisch'inna, to one of the Mill Creek villages, Tuliyani. There are only a couple of reasonable routes between the creeks in the Yahi winter range, and both climb out of Deer Creek near Iron Mountain, right about where Yisch'inna should be, and end up in the basin between Table Mountain and Long Point, which is probably Tuliyani. Several trails lead north from there today, just as they do on Ishi's map.

This would make the area around Black Rock Tolochuaweyu.

A couple of other clues can be drawn from Ishi's map. He showed two villages lying across Deer Creek from each other, upstream from Yisch'inna. This is unusual, as most Yahi winter settlements are on the north side of a stream, which gets more sun and is thus a warmer, more hospitable place when the people were there in the course of their annual migration.

But upstream from the current Ponderosa Way bridge, Deer Creek turns and runs almost due north and south. Neither side of the creek would have a solar advantage. There is a basin on the west side of the creek — Gahma, perhaps — and to the east, an area with two streams flowing into Deer Creek could be Puhiya.

Finally, Ishi said the next village upstream, K'andjau-ha, lay at the head of the salmon migration up Deer Creek. And within the next basin is Lower Deer Creek Falls. A fish ladder was built there decades ago and updated recently, but in the creek's natural state, it would have been an obstacle to migrating fish.

There are three or four obvious basins at the downstream end of Yahi country that aren't shown on Ishi's map, but that we know were home to Indians. These sites were vulnerable to raids by settlers in the Sacramento Valley and had probably been abandoned by the time Ishi was born, believed to be about 1860.

The same is true for sites farther north — in the streams up to Antelope Creek and perhaps beyond. That country is less rugged than Mill and Deer creeks, and loggers and ranchers were setting up in those areas as early as the 1850s.

Each of these villages would have been small. We don't know how many Yahi there were, but the most reasoned estimates put the population on Deer and Mill creeks between 250–450 Indians. With six winter villages identified along those streams, the average village size would have been 50–60 Indians.

Allowing for the fluctuation between large "rich" villages and the smaller ones, we can say the largest Yahi village may have numbered 80; the smallest ones, perhaps as low as 30.

Add in the villages in the basins along the streams father north and the population of the Yahi may have been as high as 750 or so at one time.

And 90 percent of them would perish in just a decade.

Chapter 4

The author and his wife Laura walk into a Yahi village site on Mill Creek in this picture taken by their son, Nate, in the 1990s.

Newcomers

For as long as there have been people in California, they have changed it for their benefit. But for the first thousands of years, the humans who shaped the land had themselves been shaped by it. They were creations of where they lived. They were part of the natural cycle of winter rain and summer fire. Their lives were lived in rhythm with the ripening of food plants, the runs of salmon, the movement of the herds, the influx of snowbirds that crowded the marshes of winter.

And while technological advances might have allowed some people to thrive at the expense of others, they did not thrive at the expense of the land. Over time the Yahi had been pressed back into their foothill sanctuary from a range that may once have reached as far south as the Sutter Buttes, east to the Big Meadows now beneath Lake Almanor, and west to the Sacramento River. But the people who supplanted them in those areas did so largely because their way of life meshed better with those lands than the Yahi way. They thrived to an extent the Yahi could not, and the Yahi had to retreat.

But in the years that we today count as the 1700s, outsiders who were very much not products of the land began to appear in California. They came with the belief that nature was something to be conquered. They sought not to adapt to California's natural cycles and resources, but rather to exploit them to further a way of life that was foreign.

Ship-borne Spanish explorers had first coursed north from Mexico along the California coast in 1542. The British explorer Sir Francis Drake followed in 1579. But the area was largely ignored for the next 200 years.

It wasn't until 1769 that the first permanent settlement was made in what is now California. A year after that Spanish foothold in San Diego, a mission and military presidio were built in Monterey, hundreds of miles north. The Spanish presence spread along the coast in the following years, culminating with construction of the Sonoma Mission in 1823, under the rule of recently independent Mexico.

By then, the Russians had built a fur trading post on the Northern California coast at Fort Ross. Three land expeditions had penetrated the Sacramento Valley, coming far enough north to sight Mount Shasta and "The Twins," which are mostly likely Lassen Peak and Brokeoff Mountain. Those peaks look like twins from the valley floor and were called the Sister Buttes into the second half of the 19th century.

It's possible a white man had penetrated Yahi country by then. John Anthony Gilbert, a Scot who seems to have accompanied the final 1821 expedition of Luis Antonio Arguello, claimed to have walked around The Twins.

At that time, a band of Spanish land-grant ranchos had spread south along the coast, but there was no permanent presence in the neighborhood of the Yahi. The outsiders were still a hundred miles away.

And for the Yahi, that was a good thing. Where the Spanish had taken root, the native populations were decimated. Indians were forced onto the missions and ranchos as laborers, charged with recreating the lifestyle of Spain on the Pacific coast. For people accustomed to living in harmony with the land, reshaping it into something different was difficult both physically and spiritually.

It was much harder work to grow the exotic crops the Spanish wanted than it was to accept the bounty the land provided. And it violated the basis of the native system of beliefs to attempt to impose human will on a countryside they viewed themselves to be part of.

There was resistance, which was beaten down with the fearsome military force of the Spanish.

The health of many natives failed in the unnatural and unfamiliar conditions they were forced to live in at the missions. They were adrift spiritually, forced to abandon their beliefs at threat of death, in favor of a Catholicism that required them to turn away from their heritage.

The best estimates are that two-thirds of the Indians in the territory settled by the Spanish died as a result of the newcomers' arrival.

But in Northern California, life continued as it had, but just for a few more years, until a new threat arrived from the north.

In 1821, the British Hudson's Bay Company had established a fur trading headquarters — Fort Vancouver — at the mouth of the Columbia River, and was sending out "brigades" of trappers to essentially kill all the fur-bearing animals in the vicinity to make the country less attractive to Americans.

Possession of the Oregon territory was then shared by the Americans and British under a vague agreement that did nothing but avert open warfare between the two nations.

The Hudson's Bay Company, in concert with the British crown, had adopted a scorched earth strategy that sought to make Oregon for the British what the Lassen foothills were for the Yahi — a land no one else wanted — by systematically stripping the attractive resources from it.

The plan broadened in 1828, when the American Jedediah

Smith staggered into Fort Vancouver from the south with the few survivors of a trapping party that had been largely wiped out by Indians.

He was returning from his second trip from Great Salt Lake to Southern California. He'd been confronted by Mexican authorities as he reached California, who told him to go back the way he had come. Instead he'd moved north, up the San Joaquin and Sacramento valleys. He'd crossed the northern mountains east of Mount Shasta and was moving up the Willamette Valley when his party was slaughtered by the Umpqua Indians, leaving just four survivors who'd been away from the camp at the time of the attack.

His arrival spurned interest in sending trapping brigades south into what was then Mexican California, which the British called San Buenaventura. They had the same basic objective: Kill enough of the fur animals to make it unattractive to the Americans.

The first brigade into California was that of Alexander Roderick McLeod, who in 1829 and 1830 penetrated the state along the McCloud River, which is named after him — phonetically — and trapped as far south as Sonoma.

And for the next decade or so, Hudson Bay brigades moved south into California through a variety of routes, one of the main ones following what's now Cow Creek through Yana territory, north of the Yahi. The trappers called the stream Canoe River, as they paused at its mouth to make dugouts to carry them down the Sacramento River.

Some trappers moved in down the coast and worked the Northern California coast ranges in the neighborhood of the Russians at Fort Ross. Those who took the inland routes trapped away from the coast, in areas where Mexican authority did not reach. They shared that part of the state with American mountain men as well.

But the enterprise was not promising. Leader of one of the brigades, John Work, reported upon returning to Fort Vancouver in October 1833 that a year's trapping had only secured 1,023 beaver pelts, and that the natives had caused trouble in the form of thefts and open skirmishes.

The Indians' hostility may have stemmed from their visitors' actions. For example, Work's brigade was trapped in the Sutter Buttes for a month early in 1833 by flooding of the Sacramento Valley that left that high ground an island. He reported during that time that his men killed 395 elk, 148 deer, 17 bear and eight antelope, "which is certainly a great many more than was required, but when the most of the people have ammunition and see animals they must needs fire upon them, let them be wanted or not."

Again, California was seeing people who did not share the natives' oneness with the land. The idea of killing unneeded game, just because you had ammunition and a target presented itself, must have been appalling.

But the devastation of wildlife was not the most serious blow to the California Indians. The trappers — Work's party particularly — brought diseases to the area for which the natives had no resistance. Upon his arrival in California, Work made note of a veritable metropolis lining the Sacramento River for most of its length, village after village of hundreds of people each. Upon his return trip north, the villages were deserted, but for the dead and those too ill to flee.

The men of Work's brigade were also falling ill from the disease they brought to the area, most likely a strain of malaria. But while the trappers were able to fight off the disease and reach Fort Vancouver, albeit terribly sick, the California natives succumbed.

A third to half of the population of the Sacramento Valley died in the pandemic the trappers brought. It's likely however that the Yahi were impacted little, due to their isolation from the valley tribes. In a way, the Yahi may have benefitted from the loss of competition for resources that came with the devastation of their neighbors.

But that devastation opened the way for another wave of newcomers, and these people came to stay.

About the time the trappers were roaming interior California — and perhaps because of Mexican authorities' inability to do anything about them — the rules on granting land to foreigners were relaxed. California was too empty to govern, and too few Mexicans were interested in settling away from the coast.

So with nothing more than an oath of loyalty to Mexico and

a claimed conversion to the Catholic faith, huge tracts of land began to be given away to Americans and others.

In Northern California, John Sutter of Switzerland started work on his fort in 1839, in what would become Sacramento. The Yahi got a neighbor in 1844, when the Dane Peter Lassen settled near the mouth of Deer Creek. Three years later there were five more ranchos in what's now Tehama County, with one in Shasta County and four in Butte County.

The land grant policy backfired on the Mexicans, because those same settlers would launch the Bear Flag Revolt in 1846. With the help of the American military, they would wrench the state away from Mexico by the following year.

The Yahi may well have been blissfully ignorant of the changes going on around them. The nearby ranchos were distant on the valley floor, lining the Sacramento River. They were huge, in the neighborhood of 20,000 acres each, ample land for whatever activities the settler might undertake without disturbing his neighbors in the hills. Each rancho was home to a band of native laborers, but they were valley Indians, with whom the Yahi had little concourse.

Still, it seems reasonable that the Yahi would have known there were newcomers in the area. It also seems reasonable that they might not have known exactly what that meant. They would learn that lesson in just a couple of years.

Chapter 5

Aerial view of The Narrows on the Lassen Trail in Yahi County. In this picture looking west, the narrow ridge drops abruptly to the right toward Mill Creek in the vicinity of Black Rock, and to Deer Creek to the left. The trail ran across the spine in between. It was just one of the many challenges on a truly awful wagon route.

1849

The most cataclysmic year in California history was 1849, the year of the Gold Rush.

In a twinkling, the soon-to-be state saw an unprecedented influx of outsiders, bent on ripping the landscape asunder to uncover the wealth hidden beneath. Mountains were moved and river courses were changed. The ecology of the state was twisted, in the course of just a few months.

For most of the California Indians, 1849 was the final disaster. Their homelands were overrun and transformed. Places where they'd lived in harmony with nature for thousands of years were reshaped into places where the old ways did not work.

The white people, who'd been the smallest of a minority, suddenly were present in numbers that could not have been imagined.

The missions had ravaged native life along the coast. The diseases of the trappers had killed many of the Indians in the Central Valley. And now the gold seekers turned the mountains into a hostile environment for the original residents there.

For the Yahi, however, a quirk of geology spared them the Gold Rush's negative impact, at least as the rush was going on.

The eastern rampart of California consists of two very different mountain ranges. The Mother Lode was in the foothills of the Sierra Nevada, which were raised by geological processes that also formed gold. The Yahi lived in the volcanic Cascade range farther north. If there ever had been gold there, it was buried thousands of feet deep beneath millions of years of volcanic mud and lava flows.

The gold fields had an abrupt north edge where the Cascades and the Sierra met. The line could be pretty well be drawn at Butte Creek Canyon, which was rich with the mineral. Big Chico Creek canyon, just four miles north, had none, and that trend continued up through Yahi country.

It was still a land no one else wanted, and the old ways could continue.

If fact, for a few years after 1849, the Gold Rush was probably a boon to the Yahi, thanks to their neighbor, Peter Lassen.

Lassen's life is a litany of bad luck, bad timing and bad judgment. There was a sequence of failed business ventures, either because they were ill-conceived or because Lassen's good nature allowed him to be victimized by his partners.

At this point, Lassen's bad timing held sway.

Gold had been discovered in January 1848, and generally, the handful of white men in California at that time became quite wealthy, quite quickly. They scooped up the easy pickings without the intense competition that would come the following year.

Lassen's past companion John Bidwell, for instance, reacted to the discovery on the American River by collecting a body of Indian laborers and heading to the Feather River. He found it also was a rich gold stream and collected a fortune in just a few months. He used the money to buy the Rancho Chico and over time, develop it into an agrarian showpiece. By the time the Forty-Niners arrived, his mining days were over, and he was living comfortably by the banks of Big Chico Creek.

But in January 1848, Lassen was in Missouri, where he lived a few years before coming to the West Coast. He had traveled back there in the summer of 1847 to talk up Benton City, the community he was planning on his Rancho Bosquejo, along the Sacramento River where Deer Creek flowed into it.

The town was named after then-Missouri Sen. Thomas Benton, perhaps because Benton's daughter was married to Capt. John Fremont, who had befriended Lassen in the period before the Bear Flag Revolt.

Over the winter, Lassen had convinced enough people to come to Benton City that in spring 1848 he led a train of 12 wagons west from Keytesville, Missouri. This was before word of the gold discovery had prompted the westward frenzy of the following year.

The transit was typical of those that were becoming more and more common at the time. The party headed up the Platte River, across the Rocky Mountains at South Pass, and west to about where the town of Winnemucca, Nevada, stands now. There, the main California Trail headed south along the Humboldt River before crossing the Sierra via Donner Pass or Carson Pass.

Lassen instead turned his party northwest, along the Applegate Trail toward Oregon. The group followed that route to Goose Lake, in the northeast corner of California, before turning south.

That's when things began to go wrong. Lassen apparently planned to use sightings of what's now Lassen Peak to navigate from Goose Lake to his ranch. It's possible he mistook Mount Shasta for Lassen Peak, as the party seemed to go farther west than necessary, diverting from an easier path south to the point Lassen wanted to cross the mountains.

The more rugged course required cutting the wagons down into more maneuverable two-wheeled carts. Supplies dwindled. And Lassen's final admission he was lost pushed the travelers to the point of threatening to hang their guide.

In the nick of time, help arrived in the form of a well-equipped party from Oregon moving south after hearing word of the gold strike. The replenished party moved on, Lassen found his bearings and the group crossed the mountains into the Sacramento Valley.

They arrived in November 1848, and found Benton City to be less than worth their trouble. Lassen's batch of potential residents bolted for the gold fields, leaving him largely alone at his community.

That might have been the end of the story for the Yahi, except the word of the gold fever was sweeping the East.

About 90,000 people came to California in 1849. The vast majority came by sea, either around Cape Horn at the southern tip of South America or via a land crossing of Nicaragua or the isthmus of Panama.

But 20,000 to 30,000 people took the land route across North America. The migration crossed the Great Plains, the Rockies and the Great Basin by essentially the same route. Near present-day Winnemuca, the first two-thirds of the Forty-Niners followed the best-known routes south and crossed the Sierra Nevada by either by Carson route, along the Carson River and Carson Pass south of Lake Tahoe, or the Truckee route, north of the lake along the Truckee River and over infamous Donner Summit.

But for some reason, on Aug. 11, 1849, one Milton McGee turned his 11-wagon train north at the Winnemuca split to follow Lassen's route. The whole last third of the migration turned to follow him, and the stage was set for disaster.

From the point where they turned off, it was about 300 miles to the gold fields by the Carson or Truckee routes. Lassen's trail added another 100 miles, and that was just to get to the Sacramento Valley.

Thus, the people at most risk of being caught in the California mountains' killing winters had opted for a route that would add a couple of weeks of travel to reach safety.[1]

It's unclear why McGee turned off. The routes to California were the topic of endless debate at the camps of people who assembled earlier that year to wait for the weather to break to head west. It's likely McGee had heard of Lassen's promotion of an easier crossing of the mountains. Perhaps he was tired of eating the dust of those who were ahead of him. Perhaps he was tired of searching for resources along a path stripped by those who had come before.

But for whatever reason, he turned, and 7,000 to 10,000 people followed.

Many of those people were at the tail of the migration for good reason. Some weren't hardy enough for the crossing. Others were carrying too much gear. Some just dawdled. Others were slowed by a lack of leadership and conflict among members. Most of them had fallen behind because they simply weren't up for the trek, and they'd just made a decision that made things worse.

Fortunately for them, about the time McGee made his turn, the authorities in California got wind of the scope of the cross-continent migration. The first migrants crossed the mountains in August and reported how many were following them. With the memory of the Donner Party debacle in 1846 still fresh, the thought of people eating people on a more massive scale prompted action.

Relief parties were assembled and sent east, first across Carson Pass and Donner Summit. What they found was the tail-end of those two groups. But scouts brought word of the great detour the last third of the migration was taken, and the rescue effort shifted north.

The first of the Lassen Trail migrants had reached Lassen's rancho by the time John Peoples arrived there to ferry supplies across the mountains to those farther behind. He moved up the trail, assessing the needs of each oncoming party and issuing bread and crackers, and beef and pork to the most desperate.

By Oct. 10, he was dispensing supplies on the Pit River. Maj. Daniel Rucker, commander of the relief effort, established a second replenishment camp in Big Meadows, another 40 miles closer to safety.

They urged the emigrants to hurry, saying winter was close, and that winter was a killer in the California mountains. Few heeded their warning. These were not the elite of the migration. With their stocks refilled, they couldn't see any urgency. Even when the rain turned to snow that night, few on the trail realized their jeopardy, because the storm was short-lived. The weather warmed afterward, and the stumbling migration continued at its deliberate pace.

The last party — the 32 men and 25 women of the St. Louis Company — staggered into the Pit River camp on Oct. 26. Most of their livestock had been run off by Indians, but they still argued on what to leave and what to carry on, despite winter's recent calling card.

Disgusted, Peoples finally put the women, children and sick into his wagons, and headed toward safety. The men followed, slowing the progress by continuing squabbles over lightening the load.

There may have been thousands of people still high in the mountains when snow began to fall in earnest Oct. 30. On and off storms hit for the next five days. Livestock died from the cold. The emigrants were caught, and in desperate straits.

When breaks in the weather occurred, people finally began

abandoning their loads and moving on quickly. Parties that had crossed the plains cooperatively shattered into individuals trying desperately to save themselves. It's a miracle there wasn't wholesale death, but that year, winter only gripped the land lightly. Virtually all of those on the trail were able to make it the Sacramento Valley and safety by Nov. 26.

All these people had walked right through the heart of Yahi country, following a ridge between Deer and Mill creeks. Yet word of interactions with the Indians is largely missing from the accounts of the Forty-Niners.

The most detailed account is *Gold Rush*, by J. Goldsborough Bruff, who spent the winter of 1849-50 in Yahi country. His Washington City Company had reached a camp in the vicinity of Barkley Mountain in the fall of '49, with their draft animals largely spent. Bruff agreed to guard the company's wagons and their loads while the rest of the crew went to the Sacramento Valley to get fresh livestock and return to complete the journey.

But as soon as the others reached the valley, they bolted for the gold fields, abandoning Bruff and their kit atop the ridge.

Bruff tended the gear faithfully for a while, but also took time to explore. He wandered one day down into Mill Creek canyon to a point where he could see and draw Black Rock. He could also see smoke curling up from Yahi villages in the canyon bottom, although the villages and their residents were hidden from view in the trees.

After a few months, Bruff left the company's train to move to a rude cabin at what's now called Obe Fields Spring that he shared with another emigrant who'd stopped there for the winter and a dog. His human companion vanished, and in the spring Bruff decided he had to move down to civilization to survive.

It was on that trip down that he reported his first interaction with what must have been a Yahi. An Indian crossed the trail ahead of him, and Bruff reported the thought crossed his mind of killing and eating the man. Instead, the two met, the Yahi shared some food with Bruff, and he continued on to Lassen's Rancho.

The incident outrages a lot of people who read Bruff's account. But in the context of the entire journal, it's clear he would not have acted on the impulse. Bruff helped a lot of people while on the trail and while watching his company's gear at what's now named Bruff's Camp. He'd shown himself repeatedly to be a selfless man of character, often doing the right thing even though he knew he was being taken advantage of.

Marker at site of Bruff's Camp on the Lassen Trail in Yahi Country.

He'd been living for the previous few weeks on candle wicks, coffee grounds and scraps of meat scraped from the stiff hides of long-dead oxen. Yes, he was eating candle wicks. It's clear from his account that he was ill and wasn't thinking clearly on his way down the hill. Indeed, he was laid up for a while after he reached Lassen's.

But Bruff's meeting on the trail is the only real account of contact with the Yahi. There were thefts attributed to unseen Indians, but it appears the Yahi just hunkered down in 1849 and watched a migration pass through that outnumbered them more than 10 to 1.

It was the only year they had to worry about, because the word of the hardship of the Lassen Trail spread thoroughly in the camps that assembled to cross the country in 1850. The route was dubbed Lawson's [sic] Cape Horn Route — a reference to the long trip around the southern tip of South America — or the Greenhorn Cutoff.

Almost no one used the trail after 1849, except residents of the Sacramento Valley who had a reason to head up to the Big Meadows or other locations in northeastern California and northwestern Nevada.

Isolation returned to the Yahi. And unlike the rest of the California Indians, the experience of 1849 left them richer. Scattered all along the trail were still-laden wagons and random items dumped to lighten the Forty-Niners' loads. It was there for the taking. And then there was the Yahi's Mother Lode: Steep Hollow.

When those on the Lassen Trail broke out of the timber into the foothill chaparral about 20 miles east of Lassen's Rancho, they got their first view down into the Sacramento Valley. At that point, the trail runs down a knife-edge ridge between Dry Creek and Boat Gunwale Creek.

But about a mile and a half from that tantalizing glimpse of the goal, a large rock formation blocked the passage of wagons. About 70 years later, the rocks were blown up by the Corps of Engineers, but in 1849, wagons could not get around them. The ridge slopes on either side of the rocks were too steep, and wagons would overturn trying to pass them.

The only solution was to follow a steep spur ridge down into Dry Creek Canyon. After dropping several hundred feet in elevation, emigrants faced a similar climb up a second spur ridge, which rejoined the ridgetop trail past the rock obstruction. That was Steep Hollow. After months of crossing the plains, many parties' livestock simply couldn't handle the climb back out of Dry Creek Canyon hauling loaded wagons. Many of the emigrants didn't have the stomach for one more struggle, with the end literally in view.

It's possible more equipment was abandoned there than made it on to Lassen's. People took only what they absolutely needed, only what they or their animals could easily carry, to attack that final barrier between them and the Sacramento Valley, and the gold beyond.

So there in Steep Hollow and to a lesser degree along the rest of the trail, what amounted to untold wealth to the Yahi had been left behind, smack dab in the middle of their country. Suddenly the Yahi had access to massive amounts of clothing, wagon canvas, boards, cooking utensils, tools, metal objects of many kinds and probably most important, bottles and glassware.

Bottle glass could be knapped into arrowheads and knives as easily as the finest obsidian, and there was no source of the volcanic glass in Yahi country. The nearest quarries were east in Mountain Maidu territory and north in Yana country, and neither produced glass of the highest grade. Now, in a glimmer, the Yahi had all they needed, right at home.

But California also had a lot of new residents. The gold would pan out, and most of those who sought it would not return home.

Rather, they'd create a new civilization on the Pacific Coast, and that civilization would spell doom for the Yahi.

Northern California Bureau of Land Management archaeologist Eric Ritter (left) points out artifacts recovered from Steep Hollow to his Shasta College field archaeology class. The items from the Lassen Trail's final challenge are housed at the Tehama County Museum in Tehama.

Chapter 6

A thunder cloud builds over Mill Creek Canyon in Yahi country.

Conflict finds the Yahi

As the new civilization around the Yahi grew, neither side was looking for a fight. But the increasing number of newcomers and their way of life, made a fight inevitable.

There was nothing in Yahi country the newcomers wanted — no gold, no farming land, no easy routes for passable roads. There was nothing worth taking. The Yahi weren't in the way like the neighboring Maidu and Wintun.

Yet there was conflict as early as 1850, over cattle that wandered into the Yahi foothills after being introduced there by settlers. Quite understandably, the placid new animals were added to the Yahi diet, a step that drew a murderous response from the settlers

In his book *Gold Rush*, J. Goldsborough Bruff reported from "Deer Valley" — probably Deer Creek Meadows — of an 1850 raid on an Indian camp on Mill Creek, "one of the ones I saw smoke curling from" near Black Rock.

Bruff suggests that raid resulted in a parlay resulting in a treaty between the Indians and the settlers that ended the theft of cattle for a time. As unlikely as that sounds, given the language differences, it may in fact have been the case, because there wasn't another credible account of a battle between the Yahi and the newcomers until the summer of 1856 or 1857.

In a January 1918 article in the *Chico Enterprise*, D.F. Crowder recounted a conversation with J.L. Keefer, a pioneer settler north of Chico. Keefer told of an annual gathering of Indians a short distance up Deer Creek canyon that was attacked in 1856 or 1857 over the killing of a steer. A stockman observed the butchering, and gathered his companions for an attack that killed a few Indians and scattered the rest.

A "bunch" of the Indians came to Keefer's and were cared for there. Crowder says one of the Indian women had a hand ruined by a shotgun blast, and Keefer cut it off with his pocketknife and bound the stump. His wife "took" a small boy named Tom as kitchen help. Indian Tom reappears in this narrative a few years later.

The Indians, Crowder said, appreciated Keefer's treatment and treated him kindly in response. Many of them stayed on as laborers on the ranch.

Robert Anderson seems to describe the same incident in his book, *Fighting the Mill Creeks*, a primary source on the destruction of the Yahi.

As he tells it, the Carter family had an Indian encampment at their ranch on Deer Creek, and used the natives for laborers. One killed a cow. In response, the Carters raised a party, sallied into the foothills and raided a camp without warning, killing several Indians at the loss of one white man.

Anderson put this raid in 1850. It's possible there were two very similar raids in the same location several years apart, but

Anderson missed on a couple of other dates that can be verified by newspaper articles or other sources. His book was written nearly 60 years after the fact, after all. It's most likely these were two accounts of the same incident.

Anderson says this attack was the cause of all the bad blood between the Yahi and the settlers. However both accounts suggest that the Indians killed were valley Indians rather than foothill Indians. Further, the Yahi would have been in the high meadows in summer, rather than low in the canyons.

While the Yahi did become much more aggressive starting in 1857, I doubt they were motivated by the attack described above. The Yahi experience with the settlers, coupled with news gathered during trade with neighboring tribes, would have made it clear the newcomers had superior weapons and little compulsion against killing. The Yahi experience up to 1857 would have prompted caution.

And yet, first-person accounts and newspaper reports from the time suggest a number of raids on the valley that winter and spring from Deer Creek northward. The Yahi must have known their actions would only escalate the danger they faced, as each attack was followed by a retaliation by the increasing population of settlers.

What might have spawned such recklessness when caution was indicated? Most likely, necessity.

The Yahi found enough in their land to live, but not much extra. When the new civilization arrived, it likely disrupted the natural system to the point the Yahi's margin for survival vanished.

Consider this: The winter and spring salmon runs were critical to the Yahi. They were probably the most essential food source they had. They came after the hardest times of winter, and filled streams with easily harvested protein after months when all that was available was dried meat, and stored acorns, nuts and seeds.

By the time the salmon crowded the streams, the people had been stretched to their limit. They were probably suffering the beginnings of the nutritional ills that come with a lack of fresh fruits, vegetables and meats. But when the salmon arrived, the Yahi were revived.

Photo from the Tehama County Library shows the Sesma Mill on Mill Creek, near its junction with the Sacramento River. By the late 1850s, there were similar water-powered mills on Deer and Antelope creeks, which may have impeded the salmon runs critical to the Yahi.

If the salmon did not arrive, many Yahi would die. And by the late 1850s, that may have been happening.

By that time flour mills had been built on Antelope, Mill and Deer creeks. The design and operation of the mills is not known, beyond that each was water-driven. Typically, that requires a dam to build up a head of water to power the grinding stones.

This was not a time when environmental impacts were considered, and the idea of mitigating the impact of the mill dams on the salmon runs would have been considered absurd. Nature was to be conquered, not protected.

There's no way of being certain that the winter and spring runs were hindered. But the time when the mills were built was the same time newspaper accounts documented the Yahi began leaving the sanctuary of the hills to raid ranches on the valley floor, even though they knew such a course of action was courting disaster. It is also clear from the news reports that the Indians were seeking food. This suggests a major disruption of the cycle that had sustained them so long.

If this theory is correct, it would be no coincidence that the raids came in late winter and early spring, about the time the surges of fish would have normally been moving upstream. And it's no coincidence that the newspaper accounts reported the raiders' preferred targets were horses and mules, protein on the hoof to replace that on the fin.

But dams weren't the only blow the newcomers inflicted on the Yahi's natural world. By the mid 1850s, logging had begun in the northern and southern reaches of Yahi country. Lumber mills were operating in the Antelope Creek drainage and on the Cohasset Ridge, in a district then known as North Point. By 1862, there were six logging mills there.

These were probably the first intrusions of full-time white residents into the Yahi's rugged range, and the results could not have been favorable for the natives. Killing Indians was regarded as a public service, rather than murder. There was profit available in abducting children for a legal Indian slave trade in the state at the time. And there was the added sick attraction of rape when women or girls were found.

These were crimes for which the culprits could not be prosecuted either, as the law prohibited the conviction of a white man on the testimony of an Indian

Even in the unlikely case that relations between the Yahi and their new neighbors were friendly, the results still likely would have proved fatal. Only a small percentage of the more than 250,000 California Indians who died as a result of contact with the newcomers were slain in cold blood. The big killer was disease. The natives had no antibodies for the germs brought into their country by the outsiders. Diseases that would make a few immigrants sick would wipe out entire Indian villages.

We know, for example, that in the early 1830s, an epidemic, probably brought by the first trappers in the area, decimated the Indians in the Central Valley. A third to a half of the population is believed to have perished. It's unknown if the influx of newcomers that followed would have been more vigorously resisted if the native peoples had been up to strength.

While the Yahi may have been spared from this first epidemic by their isolation, it's reasonable to assume that at some point after the newcomers met the Yahi, the tribe could have been similarly reduced.

Yahi culture wasn't set up to absorb the kind of blows it was taking. It was not a large, tightly linked society. The Yahi "nation" was no more than a dozen or so extended families, scattered through a handful of canyons until summer gathered them at the high meadows. Each family — each village — was separate and independent, which left each one that much more vulnerable.

It would not have been necessary to kill all the Yahi to destroy the people. With the sharp division of labor between men and women, the slaughter of a few individuals of either sex would take a whole range of foodstuffs from the survivors, and probably put them in severe straits.

Consider the case of the smaller villages. The 15 or so people probably would have had only four or five hunters: a couple of men and a few boys still developing their skills. That's few enough to be killed in a single unfortunate encounter with white men. With that, meat vanishes from the survivors' diet, likely forcing them into the care of another village.

The hunters there would be forced to capture that much more game, even though their range was shrinking with the encroachments of the newcomers. The need to hunt more often increased the possibility of fatal encounters with those pale neighbors, which further threatened the survivors.

Other factors also contributed to Yahi vulnerability. The acorn crop from the predominant oaks in Yahi country — black oaks, blue oaks and live oaks — was variable. Other foods became critical when a harvest failed.

The impact was probably highest along Deer Creek, as the Cohasset Ridge towers over most of the prime living areas along that stream, giving the new logging operations at a commanding location over the Indians living there.

The Antelope Creek drainage, somewhat less extreme than the landscape of Mill and Deer creeks, also would have become inhospitable to the Yahi quickly. It was easier to reach, which made it more vulnerable. And the location of the logging mills near current day Lyonsville would have led to a regular traffic through that watershed, a situation that must have bode ill for the Indians.

The picture is one of increasing compaction, as village after village along Deer and Antelope creeks lost the ability to support itself, and was forced to merge with others. Ultimately the survivors were forced into Mill Creek canyon, which was more remote and still relatively secure against white influence.

But there in the swollen Mill Creek villages, there must have been constant hunger and common starvation, as the natives struggled to gather more food from less land, and to cope with things like the disappearance of the salmon. It takes little imagination to understand why the Indians were forced to creep down amongst the ranches of the settlers under the cover of darkness, to search for food. It takes a better imagination than mine to find an alternative explanation.

The Yahi didn't see any difference between livestock and game, except that the new animals were larger than deer, and more docile and thus easier to hunt.

However, the white settlers didn't see it that way. The Indians were thieves who threatened prosperity and tranquility. Their "depredations" were punishable by death, with no courtroom necessary for the sentence to be carried out.

And when murder became meritorious, the Yahi's fate was sealed.

1857

In *Fighting the Mill Creeks*, Robert Anderson reported many raids on the valley early in 1857, an account seemingly supported by a September article in the *Red Bluff Beacon* referring to "the outbreak last spring." There were no articles recounting raids early in the year, but that doesn't mean they didn't happen. The only way the Beacon could have learned of a raid along Deer Creek where Anderson lived would have been if someone had taken a day off to ride into Red Bluff and report it, something unlikely to have been a priority for folks in that era.

The first newspaper accounts of attacks that year appeared in June and concerned what may have been an Indian offensive against the Antelope Mills lumber camps, about 25 miles east of Red Bluff in the Antelope Creek drainage near present-day Lyonsville. The mill was a major intrusion into Yahi territory; it was somewhat isolated and may have seemed vulnerable. It was struck twice in June and once in August, perhaps as the Yahi were heading to the high meadows and again upon their return. Several more unsuccessful threats on the mills would be reported in the *Beacon* over the next few years.

The accounts sometimes are confusing, as the newspaper gives the same name to the lumber mill in the foothills and the flour mill at the mouth of Antelope Creek canyon, about five miles out of town.

In the June 17 edition is a report that five days earlier, Indians raided a cabin in the lumber mill's vicinity. One of the residents was some distance away, and observed 75 Indians swoop down on his partner, killing him. They were said to have lopped off the dead man's arm and carried it away.

Tehama County pioneer Chris Kauffman, who later wrote a newspaper account of an attack on Yahi County in 1860 (included as an appendix to chapter 9 in this book), said that the man who was killed was John Loree, and that the severed arm became a totem of sorts for the Yahi, an object of much power. He placed the attack at "Judd Ranch, later J.C. Turner's" which is near the current Lyman Springs.

According to the *Beacon*, the survivor of the attack fled to Red Bluff, where a party of 15 formed to pursue the Indians. They tracked the culprits to Mill Creek canyon, where they attacked a "ranchero" of about 200. The Indians stood their ground, returning fire, and chased the raiding party back to Red Bluff, wounding two of them. The raiders claimed 50 Indians killed.

Another party of 50 whites formed to carry on the conflict — including the editor of the *Beacon* — but a five-day expedition failed to find any sign of the Indians. While the raiders were in the field, the Indians again struck at Antelope Mill, but did little damage.

The numbers of Indians and the casualty counts are clearly exaggerated. There aren't the resources in Yahi country to support a rancheria of 200, and a raiding party of 75 could have represented the entire male population of the tribe at the time. The inflated numbers do however make the Indians more of a threat and the white raiders much more heroic. The idea that 15 men could have killed 50 with the weapons available in 1857 is ridiculous.

In August, Indians launched another unsuccessful attack on Antelope Mills. The *Beacon* published a letter from Albert Wayland on Sept. 2 that the Indians had been detected as they approached at night by James Hopper, who shot and wounded two.

Two weeks later the *Beacon* published a report that Indians were raiding throughout the Cold Springs Valley, east of the Inskip Hills. Dr. E.W. Inskeep, for whom the hills were apparently named, had lost a couple of horses, and devised a plan to move the Indians in his district to the Nome Lackee reservation.

The reservation, the second ever in the Unites States, had been created in 1856 on the west side of the Sacramento Valley at Paskenta, about 30 miles southwest of Red Bluff, as a gathering place for Northern California tribes. For a number of reasons, it never worked. There'll be more on that later.

Inskeep's plan was derailed by the appearance of a person the Indians feared, the *Beacon* reported in a strange little account. Even though the arrival had "no evil designs" at this time, the Indians fled into the hills and resumed raiding.

It's unknown if the feared person was white or Indian. The arrival of a feared Indian killer like Hiram Good might have prompted flight, but there are recurrent accounts involving an evil "old doctor" among the Mill Creeks who was also greatly feared.

Before the year was out, two more accounts of conflict with the Indians would appear in the *Beacon*. On Oct. 14, it reported that a Mr. Alexander was driven from a hunting camp "beyond" Antelope Creek by Indians with rifles, even though he "keeps a friendly squaw to protect his camp."

Then on Dec. 23, a report attributed to Mr. Meador of Tuscan Springs said the Indians were causing trouble on Salt Creek.

Meador said the unfortunate Mr. Alexander, who'd moved his camp to within two or three miles of the springs, had been raided again, and that a band of 300 Indians was prowling in the hills.

Again, the numbers are suspect. It would be difficult for those hills to support that large a population in late December.

However inflated numbers would build support for armed expeditions into the hills come spring, a solution the *Beacon* clearly supported.

1858

This is the year in which desperation among the Yahi becomes obvious in newspaper accounts. Beginning in January, raid after raid by the Indians is reported, along with several expeditions into the hills in response.

The Indians were reported to have stolen 50 cattle in late January from settlements on Deer and Mill creeks in the Feb. 3 edition of the *Red Bluff Beacon*. A party formed to pursue the raiders but the results were not reported. On March 3, however, the *Beacon* reported a second raid of retribution by a party of 17. They found a village of 200-300 people 15 miles into the hills, the newspaper reported, with 20-25 rifles and two white men. The numbers are unreasonable, but again, would justify the raiders' lack of success.

It's unclear if that's a different raid from one reported March 11 in the *Butte Record* newspaper from Oroville. In the *Record's* account, 23 Indians were killed in Dry Creek canyon — which lies between Deer and Mill creeks — in response to the theft of some cattle at Tehama. "Such a course is to be depreciated," the paper commented, "but what are the settlers to do?"

Two other retaliations, and additional Indian deaths, were reported before summer.

From March through May several raids for food were reported in the *Beacon*. A large amount of bacon was stolen from Joseph Chafee's smokehouse. Two horses were taken from the Salt Creek ranch of Maj. Bradley and his sons. Two horses and two cows were taken from the W.H. Bahrey ranch, a few miles from Red Bluff. There was an unsuccessful attempt on the horses at the Klotz ranch. Six cattle were taken from Mr. Bacon on Antelope Creek, and another two horses from Maj. Bradley.

On March 17 the *Beacon* was reporting that 14 white men had been shot over the winter, with a dozen guns stolen. However only two killings of settlers had been detailed by that time. The newspaper actually carried two items on the attack, the first saying a Mr. Benjamin and his son had been slain near the head-waters of Paynes Creek, and later that a Mr. Allen and his son had been killed in about the same place

That coincidence is resolved by a letter Dr. Inskeep wrote to Gov. John B. Weller seeking troops. Inskeep wrote that Benjamin Allen and his son had been killed March 6 while building a bear trap in the area.

A third man with them, George Armstrong, had left about noon to cook dinner when he heard "frightful noises" from the direction he had come. He turned back and soon met the boy, shot through the body, who told him his father had been killed. Armstrong continued back toward the trap, getting close enough to see Indians stripping Allen's body. He returned to the wounded boy and took him to a brook to give him water, when he saw four Indians approaching. Armstrong headed after them, and they broke into the cover of the bush.

Armstrong placed the boy under the cover of some brush, and went for help. Upon returning, they found the boy's throat had been cut and he'd been disemboweled, Inskeep reported

Curiously, one of the *Beacon's* accounts is attributed to a Mr. Hobby, who said he escaped in a hail of bullets.

The killings were enough to prompt Gov. Weller to ask Brig. Gen. Newman S. Clarke, commander of federal troops along the Pacific, to send a force to the area.

On April 6, Clarke ordered a detachment of the 4th Infantry Regiment under the command of Capt. Henry M. Judah to Fort Reading, about 20 miles north of Red Bluff, near the current town of Anderson. When Judah and his 36 men arrived in Red Bluff April 16, he recognized the problem was there, and dropped the plan to move farther north.

At this point, one of those strange disconnections happened that were common in the federal government's relations with the Indians. Gen. Clarke also wrote to Thomas J. Henley, superintendent of Indian affairs for California, asking for his cooperation in dealing with the Antelope Indians. Henley agreed, apparently meaning that he'd accept any Indians the army brought him at the Nome Lackee Reservation. However the army apparently thought Henley was going to send an Indian agent to work with the troops and negotiate the Indians' surrender.

So when on May 7, Judah sent Lt. Hiram Dryer and 21 men up to Antelope Mills, their orders were to wait for an Indian agent who was never sent. Only if negotiations were unsuccessful was Dryer to undertake "chastisement" of warlike Indians.

Dryer passed the time with a series of explorations of the area, including a trip the length of Antelope Creek canyon which found no recent signs of Indians. He encountered a pair of white men who reported several cattle had been stolen from a ranch on Battle Creek and that a party was in pursuit, but the neighborhood of the mills was generally quiet.

Meanwhile Judah's disenchantment with the settlers was growing, fueled by a meeting May 25 in Antelope, on the east side of the Sacramento River, across from Red Bluff. Twenty-nine men signed a declaration that all the Indians north of Butte Creek on the east side of the river, and north of Stony Creek on the west side, either had to report to the reservation of face death. Settlers "with boys or girls they wish to keep" had to post bonds for the good behavior, the Beacon reported.

The group met again on June 5 and formed a company of 35 to enforce the edict, but that group disbanded "to reform in accordance with law." It's unclear what that means, and it appears there was no action that summer.

But the army had had enough of what Judah called "barbarity" and "the summary manner in which the whites in this section of country persisted in treating the Indians." Dryer was recalled from the hills and the infantry marched north on June 10, headed for Fort Jones in Siskiyou County.

The newspaper accounts of Indian raids had stopped that summer until late August, when vegetables and 15 sacks of wheat were stolen from a Mr. Riggs on the east side of the river, across from Red Bluff. A party pursued and caught up with the raiders in the Antelope Creek drainage, killing one Indian and recovering the food.

There's another account from November of an expedition to address thievery along Deer Creek. Seventeen men went into the hills and reportedly found a village 15 miles from the valley. The account says the attackers themselves came under attack, but were victorious in the end, without any of the raiders being injured. Indian casualties are not cited. It's another one of those questionable accounts, with the village put at 200 to 300 people.

The year ended quietly, if the *Beacon*'s lack of reports are indicative, with one of the few notes of interest in the last few months being the killing of a "white-headed eagle" that measured 7 feet, 5 inches from wingtip to wingtip, as reported in the Dec. 15 edition.

It was a different era.

Some of the raids reported in 1858 may not have been by Yahi. The use of firearms is one question, as Ishi apparently had no idea how those weapons worked when he came into the company of the anthropologists. There could have been a conscious decision by the last survivors of the Yahi to forgo those weapons as a means to perfect their hiding, or perhaps just a few — who perished — mastered guns.

But the lack of raids from May to August supports the idea it was the Yahi. In the period of calm, they would have been far up into the hills, in their summer range. They could well have been aggravating their Mountain Maidu neighbors in Big Meadows, but they were too far away to impact the Sacramento Valley.

The pattern resumed in 1859, but it's a year of such activity as to warrant its own chapter. And it's a year that shows that just a decade after the Gold Rush, the Yahi were on their last legs, not because of a conscious genocidal campaign, but just from the collateral damage of two unreconcilable cultures coming into conflict.

Chapter 7

Cliffs of the Devil's Den on the south slope of Deer Creek Canyon soar 60 to 100 feet straight up. A snow-covered Lassen Peak -- Waganoopa to the Yahi -- can be seen on the distant horizon.

1859

The year 1859 provides a milestone along the path of the Yahi's destruction. The newspapers were full of accounts of Indian "depredations" in the winter and spring that had settlers calling for action. And that summer and fall, that action was taken, with the federal army, state militia and an organized band of civilian vigilantes moving into the Yahi hills for extended periods.

And none of them appear to have found any Yahi.

This isn't to say the Yahi weren't there. The summertime expeditions looked most closely at the Yahi winter range, which could be expected to be empty. But dozens of armed white men moved through the high meadows at times that year with the specific goal of killing or capturing the Indians responsible for the spring raids in Tehama County. That no sign was found is telling.

Coincidentally, the first white settler in Tehama County, Peter Lassen, was killed April 29 in northeastern Nevada, probably by Northern Paiutes.

The year began as the previous two had, with nighttime raids on the valley floor east of the Sacramento River in search of livestock and other food.

The *Red Bluff Beacon* reported three horses were taken in March from Dr. Earl's home, five miles east of Red Bluff. Another two horses were taken from Job Dye early in April. Two horses, a mule team and four cows with calves were taken a couple of days later from the vicinity of current-day Los Molinos, although a pursuing party recaptured the cattle at the base of the hills.

The list grows to the point the *Beacon* at one point claimed every settler east of the river had been hit by what were "nightly excursions." One begins to wonder whether all the incidents could be laid upon the Indians. For instance a series of crop and grass fires blamed on the Indians are reported in June, but they seem quite similar to the blazes that happen in the summer in this area today.

The first expedition was mounted into the hills on April 6. Two parties headed in on either side of Mill Creek, the *Beacon* reported, but the southern force crossed to join the northern group. A village was subsequently found — on the south bank — and high water precluded a crossing and attack.

The settlers' anger was raised to a new pitch by a fire that claimed the lives of eight members of a prominent household, blamed on an Indian servant.

The story, pieced together from accounts in the *Beacon*, is that the home of Col. Edward A. Stevenson in Antelope, east of Red Bluff, burned before dawn on May 12, after the doors were locked and the keys removed to prevent escape.

Col. Stevenson's wife Harriet and their three children, Frank, 5, Emma, 3, and Wilmont, 4 months, were burned to death along with their housekeeper Mrs. Catherine Cronk and her two children, Emarilla 3, and Edward, 6 months. Mr. Cronk escaped the fire badly burned but died May 20.

Col. Stevenson's location at the time is not indicated in the newspaper accounts.

Tom, a 10-year-old Indian boy who worked at the ranch, was missing along with a horse and saddle by the time neighbors responded to the fire. A party set off in pursuit and captured him later that day a dozen miles north of Red Bluff. After some forceful questioning, he was said to have confessed.

A coroner's inquest determined the fire was arson and the deaths homicide, with Tom most likely responsible, but the case never went to formal trial.

In a classic case of frontier justice, the sheriff decided he didn't have authority to hold the boy due to his young age, and released him from jail. He was promptly hanged by friends and family of the victims.

Newspapers in Sacramento and San Francisco howled over the lynching, but the *Beacon* stood behind the locals for ridding from the world "what all agree was a monster in iniquity and bloodshed."

"... We cannot outrage the feeling of the friends and relatives of his murdered victims, and those who felt they were performing an act of humanity in putting him out of the way, by characterizing them as murderers," the *Beacon* wrote in a June 4 editorial.

Even before the fire, residents of the district had been clamoring for official action against the Indians in the foothills. Four separate letters were written to Gov. John B. Weller during May asking for some form of military action. With the fire, however, the tenor changed from seeking protection to something more.

An editorial in the *Beacon* on May 24 captured the tone: "That fairest part of our country has been, within the last few years, almost despoiled of its beauty by the heartless and fiendish operation of the tribe of Indians living in the foothills ... The Indians must be chastised; — that sort of chastisement they most merit is a total extermination of the fragment of their tribe."

On the 26th, after a two-day boat ride up the Sacramento River from Benicia, Company A of the 6th Infantry disembarked on the east bank of the Sacramento River and moved to camp at the mouth of Antelope Creek Canyon.

The troops' commander, Capt. Franklin F. Flint, sent a report to headquarters at Benicia on the 27th, detailing a meeting that day in Red Bluff with some of the "prominent citizens of the county," asking Flint if he was there to wage "a war of extermination" against the Indians.

"It is evident my orders do not meet that expectation," Flint wrote. "In fact, regular troops are not the kind of force they want. And in petitioning the Governor they expected him to respond by sending volunteers, acting against the Indians to kill them. And it appears that nothing less will satisfy them."

And indeed on the 29th, the fourth letter was sent to Gov. Weller asking not for regular troops to protect them, but for money to raise a volunteer army. Weller would respond to that request by sending the commander of the state militia to Red Bluff on a fact-finding mission in July.

But in the interim, some of the residents east of the river had taken things in their own hands, and collected money to pay a bounty on Indian scalps, the *Red Bluff Beacon* reported on April 6.

The practice seems so appalling to our modern values, but no legal authority moved to stop the effort, and eight or nine men took on the task that summer.

The scalp hunt

The group headed into the hills in June, but as the scalp hunt is described in Robert Anderson's *Fighting the Mill Creeks*, one comes to wonder whether it was more an excuse the eight came up with for spending a summer in the mountains. June, Anderson noted, was unusually hot that year, and the trip hit many of the spots Sacramento Valley residents flee to today to escape the heat.

They visited Deer Creek Meadows and Battle Creek Meadows. They climbed Lassen Peak. They killed a couple of bears. And it wasn't until the waning moments of the campaign that they killed any Indians, and the ones killed do not seem to have been a threat to Tehama County.

Anderson was joined by Hi Good, John Breckenridge (who would come to be elected captain) William Simmons, John Martin, John McCord, and two men identified only as Cartin and "Slim." Anderson says the authorities sent a Capt. Bill Burns to take command of the expedition, but he proved inadequate for the task and returned to the valley after the first day's march.

The raiders moved into Yahi county by crossing Deer Creek Flats and dropping down to Deer Creek. They crossed and climbed to the highlands between Deer and Mill creeks. Scouts were sent as far as Deer Creek Meadows. The party then moved down into Mill Creek canyon, crossed the creek and made camp part way up the north slope. Patrols went both upstream and down, and failed to find signs of any Indians.

In his book Anderson makes the implausible report there was an undetected village right under their nose at this point, creekside at the head of the ridge upon which they were camped. The Indians made themselves known by chopping down a tree to bridge Mill Creek and making their escape across the fallen log. This despite the fact Mill Creek is fordable in numerous places in June. The Indians covered their efforts with occasional potshots into the camp located uphill from them, Anderson wrote.

But Breckenridge turned up in Red Bluff in late June for provisions and to bring in a sick man, and reported to the newspaper no Indians had been found in Deer or Mill creeks, and the group was moving north into the Antelope Creek drainage.

Anderson's account does match that, saying the raiders had somehow determined the village had been largely women and children, and instead chose to follow the northbound tracks of a dozen "bucks."

The trail led to Black Buttes on Antelope Creek, and then beyond to Battle Creek Meadows. Anderson reports the mule team reached the meadows "by a devious course" which must refer to the return to the valley for resupply.

At the meadows, the raiders divided into two hunting parties while waiting for the supply train. Each tangled with a bear.

The pack train was then sent back to Black Buttes while the six armed hunters headed on, climbing to the top of "Lassen's Butte" and all the way to the Pit River, in Anderson's telling

The party, still failing to find any Indians, swung back west and south through Yana territory. They stopped at a sawmill northeast of Red Bluff that Anderson said had been just been attacked by Indians, and moved on to Black Buttes, reuniting with their train. The whole group then moved south, crossing

Mill and Deer creeks, and set up camp on the Cohasset Ridge.

It was now late July, and the hunters had been in the field over a month with nothing to show for it. Scouts moved out, and ultimately located an Indian gathering at what's now smack in the center of the community of Forest Ranch.

It was well out of the territory of the "Mill Creeks" and by most accounts, this particular group of Maidu was not a threat to Tehama County, or to Butte County where they were located for that matter. Regardless, an attack was promptly mounted.

The village was surrounded in the night, and the shooting started at dawn. Anderson reported the women were allowed to escape through the ring of shooters and says many men disguised themselves as women and fled too. Still, he reports, 40 Indians were dead on the field when the slaughter was over.

Newspaper accounts from the time differ with Anderson's death toll. Someone from the raiders apparently returned to the valley and got word to the *Beacon* that 14 Indians and one white man, presumed to be their leader, had been killed. The *Butte Record* said nine had been slain — including two women and two children — and that two had been wounded, perhaps fatally.

The attack spurred outrage over what the *Record* called a "most brutal and atrocious wholesale slaughter of Indians." The Indians who were killed were peaceful, and the attack was unprovoked, correspondents reported.

Anderson and the other raiders loaded themselves up with booty and headed back down to the foot of the Cohasset ridge. Survivors of the massacre pursued them, firing from long range with little effect. Indians, probably the same ones, later ambushed two teamsters farther up Cohasset ridge, seriously wounding William Lindsey.

The raiders dallied at their camp for a time, being reinforced by 15 men out of Chico under the command of Conrad "Coon" Garner. They marched back to the massacre scene and went on to the mining camp of Forks of Butte, then the nearest town to the slaughter, where they were met with hostility. They backed off, took several captives in Butte Creek Canyon, and returned to Rock Creek, where the prisoners promptly escaped.

The white war party, which now numbered over 20 men, took one more shot at the Indians. Most of the men moved up the Cohasset ridge, and then east to Cold Springs, while scouts combed the surrounding countryside. Anderson and Ad Williams went to Deer Creek and headed up that stream, finding a village on the south side of the stream, probably in the vicinity of Puhiya.

The whites moved to surround the village, but rough terrain didn't allow them to complete the effort before dawn. The trap was sprung before it was set, and many of the Indians escaped upstream. Several were killed, and others were taken captive.

It is significant that several of the captives were known to the raiding party. One, a "dangerous and troublesome customer" named Billy, was subsequently executed after he admitted shooting Lindsey.

Our understanding of the Yahi is that they kept separate from their Indian neighbors, to say nothing of the whites. That the raiders knew an Indian by name would suggest that he was not a Yahi.

Further, the account indicates the village may have consisted of Maidu survivors of the massacre a few days earlier, just a few miles south. Yet they were well into Yahi territory. Breckenridge would go as far as to later tell the *Beacon* that all the depredations on Deer Creek had been done by Butte Creek Indians, assisted by miners along that stream.

This suggests the Yahi were no longer able to secure their borders. We don't know if there were Yahi at the village who had admitted outsiders, or just Maidu. The repression common in Maidu territory at this time might have prompted a migration to the seeming security in more rugged lands which had once been Yahi, but were now left vacant by the decline of the original residents.

Anderson and his party took their prisoners to the Nome Lackee reservation west of Tehama and returned to their homes — or in Anderson's case, the ashes of his home. His ranch and one belonging to a neighbor had burned on Aug. 1, with the arson blamed on the Indians.

On Aug. 31, the *Beacon* reported the results of a long talk with Breckenridge in which he said the raiders had killed 29 Indians, "only three or four of them women or children," and taken another 13 women and children to the reservation.

But by then, yet another party of raiders had headed into the Yahi hills.

Kibbe's campaign

On June 29th, the *Beacon* was reporting Indians had killed and mutilated a teamster named William Patrick, who was hauling hay between Cold Spring Valley and Antelope Mills, perhaps a dozen miles from the federal troops camped on Antelope Creek. Another man was reportedly attacked in the same area by 13 Indians but was able to escape.

Not surprisingly, the newspaper editorialized about the "total insufficiency" of Flint's command and called on the governor for a state-backed military campaign.

In this era, the states and federal government each had separate military authority, and California often used its power due to a philosophical difference over the "Indian Problem."

When federal troops were sent to an Indian outbreak, they typically found the situation less dangerous than the locals had suggested, and often concluded it was the Indians who needed protection from the settlers rather than the other way around. For example, Capt. Flint had reported after arriving in Red Bluff that there was no evidence the Indians had committed the depredations in the area.

The state, on the other hand, wanted the Indians out of the way, by whatever means necessary. The prior year, a group of state-sponsored "rangers" had swept the area along the Trinity River. Elsewhere in 1859, another group rampaged in the area surrounding the Nome Cult reservation in Round Valley, earning a reputation for brutality.

And in late July, commander of the state militia Adjutant Gen. William Kibbe arrived in Red Bluff to see if an expedition should be mounted into the Tehama County foothills. That was probably a foredrawn conclusion.

On Aug. 10, the *Beacon* carried an advertisement by Kibbe seeking not more than 80 men for a campaign against "the Deer Creek and Antelope Indians."

"None but men inured to the hardships of mountain life, and experience with the use of the rifle required," the ad continued.

Ten days later, 75 "Kibbe Rangers" marched east out of Red Bluff for a three-and-a-half-month campaign that would leave as many as 200 Indians dead and perhaps another thousand forced from their homes to distant reservations.

And although the force was nominally formed to end the threat of the Indians in the Tehama foothills, very few of those killed or captured were taken from that area.

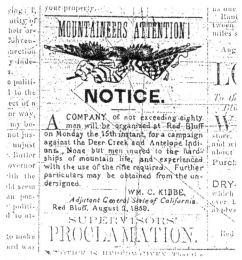

California militia chief William Kibbe's ad in the Aug. 10, 1859, edition of the *Red Bluff Beacon*, seeking volunteers for a campaign against the Yahi. Image captured from microfilm.

The effort was joined by 27 men assembled in Chico under the command of Coon Garner. That group cooperated with Kibbe, but it's unclear if they operated under his franchise. Two other shadowy forces — the Pit River Rangers and a company raised near Shasta city — also entered the picture but they were were not under Kibbe's authority.

Two federal units were also in the area. Capt. Flint's regulars were in camp east of Red Bluff, and the *Beacon* reported 50 of the 60 men there were sick. Company A of the 1st Dragoons were at Fort Crook on the Pit River and actually confronted Kibbe's force at one point, but were forced to stand down due to the superior numbers the state brought to the field.

It was the largest military campaign ever mounted in the territory between the Pit River and the Feather River, but little is known about Kibbe's campaign. Anderson dismissed it with a few sentences in *Fighting the Mill Creeks*, and Kibbe's own official report on the operation doesn't help, as it's long on platitudes and short of details — except for putting the cost at $49,468.43. Ernest Neasham's book, *Fall River Valley*, includes valuable materials on the later phase of the campaign, but no single source ties it all together.

However the newspapers of the day, particularly the *Beacon* and the *Shasta Courier*, carried extensive reports, including the accounts of correspondents among the men in the force. These allow us to trace the course of the campaign.

It began as one would expect, if the objective were in fact clearing the Tehama foothills. A northern column under Lt. Robert Bailey moved due east and reached Battle Creek Meadows by Aug. 29 without incident. In the center, Capt. William Burns (his name also appears as Byrnes) and 25 men moved up the Lassen Trail. On Aug. 24 they swept down on the survivors of Breckenridge's raid on Deer Creek and took the Indians captive without bloodshed. The prisoners were marched west under guard to be taken to a reservation.

They were the last people captured in Yahi country, because other issues had become more pressing. Breckenridge's excursion into Butte Creek had riled up both the white and native population in that area, and trouble was brewing far north along the Pit River.

Kibbe accompanied the southern column under Lt. Van Shell as it moved to the north end of the Cohasset ridge. That group would follow a rough route that would bring them down on Forks of Butte from the north, while Garner's men came up Butte Creek canyon from the west.

Along the way, Garner raided an Indian village a half-mile from Centerville, killing three Nimshew Maidu and taking 10 or 12 prisoners. Garner left four men — including Breckenridge — to guard the prisoners, and moved on to meet Kibbe and Van Shell further upstream. The angry residents of Centerville secured the assistance of a deputy sheriff and arrested the four guards, setting the Indians free. Kibbe interceded, and ordered the four whites released. There's no report of what happened to the freed Indians.

In the meantime, Van Shell's and Garner's men were gathering up Indians in the vicinity of Forks of Butte, and shipping them off to the reservation with a guard under the command of a Lt. McCarthy.

In early September Van Shell and Burns reunited in Butt

Valley. As most of the force recuperated, a detachment under Kibbe's commissary officer, S.D. Johns, moved south along the West Branch of the Feather River. They seized Kimshews,

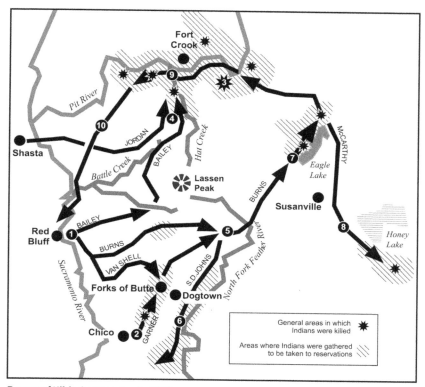

Events of Kibbe's campaign in 1859
1) Aug. 20: Kibbe and 75 men leave Red Bluff.
2) Late August: Butte Creek Nimshew Maidu are rounded up to be sent to a reservation. Several were later freed by a mob of whites from the area.
3) Sept. 3: "Pit River Rangers" attack a village on Beaver Creek and massacre 75 Indians in retaliation for the killing of four or five white men on Hat Creek and the Pit River.
4) September: Kibbe takes Lt. Bailey's men north in response to the violence there.
5) Early September: Burns' and Van Shell's men unite in Butt Valley.
6) Mid-September S.D. Johns sweeps south along the Feather River and gathers several hundred Maidu to be taken to a reservation.
7) Early October: Attacks on Eagle Lake leave dozens of Indians dead.
8) October-December: Lt. McCarthy leads a force south to Honey Lake that kills dozens of Indians and take 33 prisoner.
9) October-November: Kibbe's men and local volunteers rampage through the Pit River and Hat Creek valleys, issuing ultimatums that see dozens of Indians killed and hundreds captured to be taken to reservations.
10) December: Kibbe's force disbands in Red Bluff.

Konkaus and "Tigers" and took them to Red Bluff. Johns arrived there on Sept. 24 with 218 Indians, not counting children.

Thus far, about 250 to 300 Maidu had been taken from their homes, and were being shipped to the Nome Cult Indian Farm at Round Valley in the Coast Ranges, or the Mendocino Reservation on the coast. The only bloodshed in the southern phase of the campaign were the casualties during Garner's move up Butte Creek Canyon. The picture was already quite different in the north.

A few days before Kibbe moved into the hills, word had come down to Red Bluff of the murders in mid-August of John Callahan and a boy, John Rizer, during an Indian raid against the Hat Creek stage station on the road from Red Bluff and Shasta to Yreka. On the 20th of the month, Napoleon McElroy and David Welch were slain at a bridge and road they were building at the Pit River, farther up the same road. Samuel Burney — namesake of the town of Burney — and an Indian boy had been killed a few miles farther west back in late March or early April.

The raids were blamed on a Hat Creek chief the whites dubbed "Shavehead." As the weeks went by, Shavehead would become the scapegoat for all of the Indian attacks from Butte Creek to the Pit River, Honey Lake to Red Bluff. In the reports, his band would grow to 60 to 80 warriors, gathered together from several tribes.

The news of the killings in the north came too late for Kibbe to revise his original plan. But necessity forced a change before the month of September was very old.

Although a cavalry detachment from Fort Crook headed out in a systematic search of the Indians guilty of the murders, some of the settlers favored a less precise solution.

Frank McElroy, one of the slain men's brother, arrived in the area with a few men seeking blood. They were joined by others from among the scattered settlements along the Pit River and Hat Creek. The party was drawn from the underside of local society. An observer, C.H. Manning, later described them as "men of the roughest character ... whose white skins covered hearts as black, and natures as savage as the red men they sought to destroy."

Among them was Sam Lockhart, a rough character who'd been waging a one-man war against the local Indians since they'd killed his twin brother, Henry, two years earlier. There's even some suspicion Lockhart might have killed McElroy and Welsh, as the toll bridge they were building across the Pit River would have put Lockhart's adjacent ferry out of business.

The Pit River Rangers, as the company called itself, conducted a few cursory patrols and some dedicated drinking for a few days, before reeling drunkenly out of town Sept. 2 en route to Beaver Creek, where white settler John Rolfe had a camp of Achomawi laborers on his ranch.

The 22 Rangers formed a half-circle around the village during the night and attacked the harmless Indians at dawn on Sept. 3. About a dozen Indian men fell in the initial shooting before the remainder escaped. The women and children remained cowering in the village, trusting in past assurances that white men didn't conduct indiscriminate slaughter of innocents.

That was not the case this time.

The white war party swept down on the women and children with hatchets and revolvers, and murdered dozens of them. The reports on the massacre put the Indian death toll between 60 and 90, only a handful of whom were men.

There was only one white fatality: Frank McElroy. One report says his actions against the Indian women and children were so extreme that he was gunned down by several of the other white raiders. Another version of his death states he stood up to charge into the village just as a drunken Ranger behind him fired off a load of buckshot. Six pellets hit McElroy in the back, mortally wounding him.

The attack evoked a hue and cry of outrage from throughout Northern California. Capt. Adams, commanding the dragoons at Fort Crook, drafted an order for the arrest of Capt. John Langley, commander of the Rangers. But Kibbe arrived on the scene first.

When the word of what was happening in the north reached him, Kibbe moved to take command of Lt. Bailey's force, then encamped at Battle Creek Meadows. He took it north through the Hat Creek Valley and arrived in time to impose himself between the U.S. troops and the raiders. Another 24 irregulars arrived to support Kibbe at about the same time. They were Capt. Jordan's Pine Grove Rangers, recruited from the rougher element around Shasta city that had a hankering to shed some Indian blood.

The federal troops were vastly outgunned. When Kibbe ruled Langley's actions justifiable, Capt. Adams had no choice but to defer to the state official.

Adams summoned back a detachment under Lt. Carr from the Honey Lake Valley, and convinced headquarters to order Capt. Flint's infantry to march from Red Bluff to Fort Crook, possibly in an attempt to reassert federal control over the Pit River region. Flint's men arrived in such poor condition that they were promptly sent back to the Central Valley, and in fact retreated all the way to the federal headquarters at Benicia before October was over.

The dragoons could do little for the rest of that season but patrol the roads in the area, staying out of the way as Kibbe's force worked over the valley.

The force at Butt Valley now received an order to move north and help. Capt. Burns divided the force into three parts, with Lt. Van Shell leading the way. The force moved through the Big Meadows (now flooded under Lake Almanor) and on to Eagle Lake, arriving Oct. 4. A series of cursory negotiations followed by bloodshed ensued. When Kibbe returned to Red Bluff for provisions on Oct. 10, he said Van Shell's men had killed "quite a few" Indians, taken many more prisoner, and burned all their rancherias.

At some point, a detachment of 18 men under Lt. McCarthy headed south to the Honey Lake Valley to deal with some "depredations" there. By mid-October, a dozen Indians had been captured and two dozen killed in that vicinity. McCarthy wouldn't come out of the hills until Dec. 14, when he arrived in Oroville with 33 prisoners, bound for the reservation.

Kibbe reassembled the bulk of his force on the Pit River by mid-October and began a five- or six-week campaign through that valley. The accounts grow sparse here, speaking of numerous engagements, with 40 Indians killed here, 15 to 20 killed there, "several" killed elsewhere. In a summary at the end of the campaign, Kibbe reported 200 Indians killed in the northern phase of the campaign, but it's not clear if that included the Beaver Creek slaughter.

Kibbe's approach appears to have been to first secure a meeting with representatives of Indians in an area. He'd then make a speech through a translator that a witness paraphrased for the *Beacon*.

There are good and bad white men, good and bad Indians, Kibbe said. Some whites treated Indians badly; some Indians would kill whites and steal their property. Therefore, Indians and white men could not live together. And therefore, Kibbe concluded, the Indians would have to leave.

This speech was delivered somewhere in the valley of the Pit River, an area that had been home to as many as 3,000 Achomawi and Atsugewi for thousands of years. There may have been a few dozen white men living in that valley in 1859, with the deepest roots going down half a decade.

And yet, Kibbe believed in all sincerity that the Indians should leave their homes to make way for the white newcomers. And he had the force to press his opinion.

And so it went for a month and a half. An unsuccessful parley, followed by the surrounding of a village in the dark and an attack at dawn, usually with a shouted order to surrender first. Many of the Indians so confronted did give up, judging from the figures quoted at the close of the campaign. Others surrendered due to the destruction of stored food supplies, which left them helpless against winter. One source says Kibbe's men led 400 Indian captives out of the north, bound together with rope nooses around their necks. Another puts the number at 533, still another at 700. The *Beacon* reported 650 camped under guard at Red Bluff in early December, although the total had dwindled down to "upwards of 400" when the time came to ship them out.

Among the prisoners were "Shavehead" and his sister "Hat Creek Liz," said to be a leading counselor for the Atsugewi who lived along Hat Creek. They were taken without a struggle, which would seem to contradict his reputation as the source for all the white men's troubles in the region.

It was decided to send the captives to the Mendocino Reservation on the north coast at Fort Bragg. The nearby Nome Lackee Reservation had proven to be too close to the Indians' homelands, and they tended to return to their former haunts.

The Nome Cult Farm in Round Valley was also not a good option, as another state-sanctioned band of rangers under William Jarboe was on the warpath in the vicinity. "He has, of course, been compelled to kill great numbers, but has not made an indiscriminate slaughter," a correspondent from Round Valley wrote to the *Beacon*.

The Indians were placed on ships and carried to the coast. Ultimately that reservation and Nome Lackee would be closed down, with the remaining residents concentrated at Nome Cult.

Postscript

The newspapers grow quiet of accounts of raids with the conclusion of Kibbe's campaign, but Anderson reports a couple of additional occurrences that winter. The first time came after a raid struck Hi Good's corral on Deer Creek, driving off cattle belonging to Good and Anderson. The pair enlisted the support of "Bully" Bowman and headed out in pursuit.

The trail of the stolen cattle wasn't hard to follow as it headed up Dry Creek. Near the head of the creek, the pursuers gained sight of the raiders across a ravine, butchering a cow.

The whites opened fire, but this time, got the worst of it. As the Indians returned fire, Good was hit in the thigh. Regardless — Anderson says — he and Bowman charged the Indian camp and drove them off, recapturing four oxen. They returned to Good and helped him back down to the valley, driving the four animals before them.

Good's injury was just a flesh wound, and it apparently healed in time for a second expedition at Christmas time.

Good, Anderson and one of the Carters headed up Deer Creek then, on the thought they might find a winter camp somewhere along that stream. But the canyon was empty. The trio finally abandoned the search to climb to Bruff's camp. A storm hit, and Anderson decided to return to the valley to catch a Christmas dance. Good and Carter chose to head down into Mill Creek canyon, continuing the search for an Indian camp.

Good and Carter were unsuccessful in Mill Creek as well, though they didn't spend much time searching in the foul weather. However while heading for home, Anderson stumbled upon an Indian band taking shelter from the downpour in a cave along Dry Creek. Anderson fled, and the Indians chose not to pursue.

This was the pattern the Yahi faced that winter. Each raid for food might draw a murderous white response. And even if they didn't raid, there was no peace for the Indians, as many living in the valley regarded Indian hunting as a recreation, something to do when you've got a break at Christmas time.

A large ragged rock formation soars from the floor of Deer Creek Canyon.

Chapter 8

Black Rock in Mill Creek Canyon. According to an account by a participant, the Yahi gathered here to surrender in 1860, but were attacked instead.

1860: The Black Rock Massacre

In the Tehama County Library in Red Bluff there is a scrapbook that was started by Superior Court Judge Herbert South Gans in his youth. The exact years of its collection are uncertain, because like many young scrapbookers, Gans did not record the date or source of his clippings.

The most fascinating item includes the only published account I have seen of an attack on a Yahi camp at the base of Black Rock in February or later in 1860.

As you research the Yahi, you stumble across oblique

references to a massacre at Black Rock, but most histories bunch it into the Three Knolls massacre or another slaughter that will come up later in this book.

This is clearly neither of those attacks.

There is nothing I have found in the newspapers of 1860 that reports it, although as I have said, that is not an indication it did not happen. Newspapers of the era relied on folks coming into the office and telling them when they conducted raids like this. In this case, the attackers may have returned to a week of neglected chores more important than riding into Red Bluff to spread the news.

And at that point, there was another reason for the participants to hold their tongues: February 1860 was the month of the infamous Indian Island massacres on California's North Coast.

On the night of Feb. 26, 1860, white men from Eureka and the surrounding area paddled canoes out to the island in Humboldt Bay where an annual ceremonial gathering of Wiyot Indians was taking place. The attackers used hatchets and axes to hack 60 to 70 Wiyot to death, almost all of whom were women and children. The men were off gathering provisions for the following day's events.

The massacre drew almost universal disgust and widespread condemnation, and the Tehama County raiders may have thought better of reporting their attack for fear of comparison to the other.

But years removed, the story could be told.

The account is written by C.F. Kauffman, member of a pioneer Tehama County family. It was clearly printed in a Red Bluff newspaper, and the year of publication can be determined to be 1882. Unfortunately the extensive microfilm collections of Red Bluff newspapers at both the Tehama County Library and the Chico State University Meriam Library have a mysterious gap that includes the year 1882.

The lack of a firm provenance bothered me, but I've gotten over it. There's really no reason to discount Kauffman's tale just because we don't know exactly when and where it was originally published.

Because in many ways, Kauffman's story seems credible. For one thing, numerous participants are named. They or their families could have called out the author if the account was fictional. And they might have been motivated to do so, because the attackers aren't made out to be a heroic band of steeled Indian hunters. Instead they bumble their way into Yahi country and succeed in launching an attack in spite of themselves.

En route, the band was spooked by a owl call in the night and fled to a snowbank, for reasons Kauffman still can't understand after 22 years. Later, the old pioneer whose common sense brought an end to the owl rout was asked to confirm that a plume of smoke seen rising from the base of Black Rock ... was in fact smoke. The final attack was started not by a sharpshooter picking off a victim, but by an accidental rifle discharge.

These aren't the stalwart mountaineers of say, Robert Anderson's yarns. These are real people, and in my mind, the account becomes more believable because of that.

Everyone can make their own judgment: Kauffman's verbatim account follows this chapter. For my part, I buy it. At least most of it.

Kauffman's tale

The story starts with a superintendent of the one of the lumber mills near present-day Lyonsville riding down Paynes Creek in February 1860, recruiting men to wage a campaign against the "Nosea" Indians.

It sounds like Kauffman is using the "Nozi" name that Stephen Powers cited for the Yana in his 1877 Tribes of California, though Powers had a different name — "Kombo" — for the Yahi.

The idea of attacking the Nosea/Yahi apparently struck a chord as 24 men gathered at Finley Lake at the date given for the rendezvous. The following day they split up, with Kauffman's group of 16 moving southeast. The remaining eight and the pack train followed on a different path. The idea was reach Mill Creek a few miles apart, with the group including Kauffman then sweeping the canyon downstream toward the others.

However it appears Kauffman's band hit the canyon rim a bit downstream from Black Rock, where the telltale column of smoke revealed the Indian camp location.

The raiders made their way down to the stream and divided

again. Kauffman and seven others forded to the south bank, and the two parties moved up canyon on both sides of the creek. The plan was to get into the two parties into position on either side of the camp and launch a coordinated attack upon it upon the discharge of a signal shot by those on the north bank.

But one of Kaufmann's group, after first taking aim at a group of Nosea atop Black Rock, then extended his rifle toward another who walked out of the encampment toward the group. Again the rifleman was talked out of firing, but as he withdrew his weapon through the brush, the trigger or hammer snagged, and the gun discharged.

With that, the attack was on.

A few shots were exchanged with the Indians on the top of the rock as Kauffman's group rushed forward. And here he includes one of those details that adds to the story's credibility for me.

Typically in accounts of raids like this, the attackers pour perfect storms of lead into the Indian camps. But that couldn't be the case in 1860. The most common rifles in this era were single-shot muzzleloaders. Once fired, the tedious reloading process would be required before the gun could be fired again. The storm of lead would be more like intermittent showers.

And that's what Kauffman describes. He notes a few of the raiders "reserved" their shots and were able to continue the attack, but those who'd fired had to stop and reload.

When Kauffman reached the "rancheria" at the south base of Black Rock, the fight had moved down slope to the creek and across. He and the others followed and found the trap had worked almost as planned. The Nosea had been chased into the gunsights of the group north of the creek, and they had inflicted heavy casualties.

When the gunfire ceased, the party found itself with a 6-year-old boy as a captive. He was assigned to Kauffman. After the group made a few more unsuccessful scouts in search of survivors of the raid, they headed home. Kauffman took the boy to his father's ranch, where he still lived. The boy was given the name of "Dick" and became one of the family for a few years.

And indeed, the 1860 Census taken a few months later does record a 6-year-old Indian boy named Dick in the Kauffman household.

At this point, the narrative changes direction to the things Dick allegedly told the Kauffmans over the next few years.

Among them was that the Nosea were gathered at Black Rock at the time of the attack to surrender and be taken to the reservation. They had heard of Kibbe's campaign the previous year, and surrender apparently seemed a more desirable option than the attrition they were suffering as civilization pressed closer and closer, and hit harder and harder.

Kauffman theorized the Indians knew his group was coming from the start, as a scout had been sighted from the Finley Lake camp. The attackers were allowed to come close with the thought that Kibbe's practice of first asking for surrender and then attacking would be followed in this case.

Kauffman laments that had the raiders known, they could have saved a number of settlers' lives, as he attributes the raids of the Mill Creeks to the survivors of the attack. They had the opportunity to clear the canyon peacefully, and end the bloodshed for good.

But for a time, the attack did end the bloodshed in that part of the country. There are no newspaper accounts for the next two years of Indian attacks in eastern Tehama County. The only contact reported came in August 1860 when a group of miners were run off Mill Creek, eight miles from Battle Creek Meadows.

The following year, the *Red Bluff Beacon* reported June 27 that "Doll and Myrich" were scouting sites for cabins in Battle Creek Meadows, and that the Rawson brothers had taken most of the valley as sheep range. The Tehama County Genealogical and Historical Society's 2007 history of Tehama County reports the Rawsons — Hi and C.B. — along with partner G.W. Grayson, had moved into the meadows in 1860.

It was the deepest penetration of Yahi country to date, and it wasn't challenged.

The Yahi appear to have begun practicing the art of staying hidden. Raiding brought retribution. Surrender was apparently not an option. Separation and isolation was the only path. With the tribe reduced in numbers by several years of warfare, they were apparently able to find a few little corners of their land where they could avoid their new neighbors, and the violence that came with contact.

Chapter 8 appendix

Aerial view of Black Rock, looking north. Mill Creek winds behind the rock, and can be seen in the shadow of the rock at lower left. According to C.F. Kauffman's account, the Yahi had gathered to surrender in February 1860, on the saddle visible to the right of Black Rock. Instead, a group approaching through the area at the bottom of the photo attacked, chasing the survivors across Mill Creek, where more gunmen awaited. Kauffman attributed the story to a boy who had survived the attack and was taken in by the Kauffman family

Kauffman's account

This article, from the scrapbook of Tehama County Judge Herbert South Gans, was cut from a Red Bluff newspaper in 1882, when the future judge would have been about 9 years old. As the prior chapter states, Northern California microfilm collections of Red Bluff newspapers have a gap that includes the year 1882, so the exact date and source of publication cannot be determined at this time.

The original scrapbook has been locked away, but a copied and reformatted version is available in the records depository of the Tehama

County Library in Red Bluff. Some spelling corrections have been made from the original, and a number of long paragraphs have been broken up to ease reading. No other changes have been made.

THE NOSEA INDIANS

A Reminiscence of Sierra Township, Tehama County

BY C. F. KAUFFMAN

In the month of February, 1860, George Denton came riding down Paynes Creek from Job Dye's saw mill, drumming up recruits to advance on the Nosea tribe of Indians, whose stronghold was that of Mill Creek Canyon. The depredations committed by this nomadic race of aborigines had become unendurable to the settlers.

Our lives seemed to be jeopardized by their actions; John Loree, John Corby, Maycon, William Patrick, a Mr. Allen and his son, all had recently been murdered by this cave-dwelling band of copper-colored natives, who would traverse our portion of the county, kill cattle, steal horses, rob dwellings, murder our neighbors, then quickly fall back to this vast canyon, with its perpendicular walls of lava and basalt.

Denton instructed us to repair to the lake, (where now Wm. Finley has a ranch on the road leading to Belle Mill) upon a given day with arms, blankets and provisions, it being the point designated as our rendezvous.

Every man upon the creek that could possibly leave home obeyed his instructions to the letter. Late one evening we gained the shore of this little sheet of water, whose glossy bosom was lit up by the camp fires of those that had preceded us. We found 19 men in camp. Our accession of five made a total of 24 able and willing persons to penetrate, to many of us, the great unknown, to avenge the deaths of our murdered neighbors.

Doctor Inskip was chosen commander-in-chief, he being familiar with the habits of these Indians, and having a more intimate knowledge of this portion of the country than any white man living east of the Sacramento at that time.

After counciling in camp, so as to particularize our course of action, the result of council was as follows: The doctor should take seven men with the pack animals along the south prong of Antelope, via Buck's Flat, thence south to Mill Creek; whilst the remaining 16, with Denton as captain, would bear farther east, striking the creek higher up, thence scour the canyon downward until we found Inskip and party.

Next morning we bid adieu to our supply train and struck across the many prongs of Antelope, passed through the "Saddle in Ridge," that which the Sierra Lumber company's high trestle now spans, and consumed the entire day in gaining a high and prominent timbered ridge.

At dusk we encamped for the night upon the divide between Antelope and Mill creeks. When we had partaken of supper and lain down with our feet toward the fire, expecting to enjoy a night's rest after our march, Tom Glenn suddenly and abruptly threw his blankets to one side. grasped his gun and exclaimed:

"Boys, away from the fire. Quick! The Indians have surrounded us!"

Instantly we left our beds and retreated to a snowdrift 100 yards from the fire. What induced us to halt at this point and endeavor to hold the bank of snow has ever since been a question that none of us could solve, unless it was to make us more discernible as objects for Indians to shoot at.

Nevertheless here we stood, chattering and shivering, when "Uncle Ben," from Shasta County, took Glenn to task as to what he'd heard. At this instant an owl hooted — "There," replied Tom, as another hoot rang out upon this dark night and in this silent forest.

Warren Wood, head sawyer from Dye's mill, sustained Glenn by saying: "Tom Glenn is right. The Indians on Pit River played the owl dodge on us, when I was with General Kibbe and, by thunder! They won't get away with it here."

"I'm going back to roost," said Uncle Ben, walking off; we all followed excepting Glenn and Wood, who soon after came and also turned in for the rest of the night.

Without breakfast and by the time we could see, our party next morning was marching on. Two miles on, at sunrise, we suddenly came upon a fearful precipice: We halted and gazed over the yawning abyss, making the brain reel and the heart grow sick. Here a most magnificent view presented itself, attracting the attention of all. In silence we took in the scene. The east seemed to have given away — our position was nearly 2,000 feet vertically above the creek and about 1,500 feet above the apex of Black Rock, which made the central figure in this, one of nature's grandest, wildest pictures.

From the side of the rock we saw a column of smoke issue. At this juncture our captain cried, "Down! Down! I see smoke."

We obeyed; then the captain motioned Uncle Ben to his side, for the purpose of exacting his opinion as to the genuineness of that column of vapor; the same being paramount to the entire company -- with the captain since the owl scare of the past night.

Memory at this writing calls to mind Uncle Ben, that silver-haired hunter and gallant old pioneer, going on all fours to the verge of the cliff, adjust his spectacles, then gaze slowly down into this vast trough of the earth; and we waited his decision in breathless silence, which finally came as follows:

"Boys, there's a nest of 'em, sure. I've seen smoke for just about 65 years, and I pronounce that the clear quill."

The smoke was evidently created by a camp of Indians. Our next move was to descend the cliff, the smoke our objective point, which increased in volume and density. We converted a tree into a ladder, which grew against the wall, by stepping into the top, lowering ourselves through its branches, then sliding down the trunk for a distance of 25 feet; thence through a causeway that led into a very steep ravine, which afforded both cover and passage to Mill Creek, where we again divided our force — eight volunteering to cross and attack from the south side of the stream, the other eight to proceed up the north bank with the understanding they fire a signal gun.

Those of the number now living that forded this cold and rapid stream, deep to our armpits, with clothing and accouterments over head, twenty-two years ago, must surely have a distinct recollection of the cutting sensation produced upon our naked bodies.

We made a hurried toilet after breasting the stream and quickly sped on toward this colossal rock that was forever looming up before us like some gigantic ghost or Cyclopean sentinel guarding this wild and inhospitable canyon, with its equally wild and inhospitable, but doomed race of people.

From the ford to the rock, the distance is about one mile. Ridges coming abrupt to the creek compelled us to scale their crests. In crossing several the dense brush required the personification of so many quadrupeds.

While traveling in this shape we discovered six Indians on the pinnacle of the rock. The Nosea tribe always had one or more of their number on the lookout; and surely must have known of our presence in their country.

We succeeded in getting within two hundred yards of the rock's base, and halted beneath a cluster of live oak trees waiting for the signal to charge. The Indians on top of the rock acted unconcernedly. We could plainly see their gestures from our place of concealment. They would at intervals throw small detached pieces of rock down from their lofty perch.

I will remark here, had our party known the intention of the Nosea tribe of Indians at this moment, many valuable lives could have been saved subsequently from the horrors of Indian butchery; for it is evident that this tribe were the aggressors in the deaths of Mrs. Dersch of Bear Creek, Shasta County, Mr. Allen's family above Millville, The Hickcock children, McCarty, while hauling lumber from Klotz's mill, also a man named Stone, killed on the Lassen Trail in 1861, and Mrs. Dikeman, who was murdered at her home on Singer Creek, south of Deer Creek.

Jim Adams was eager to fire at those overhead. We, however, prevailed on him not to do so. After an interval of a few moments that seemed like hours an Indian came walking around the east side of the rock, a deer skin over his shoulders, and sat down fronting us at a distance of 175 yards. Again Adams leveled his gun, whispering: "Oh! How I could plug him!" Again we remonstrated, but in drawing back his weapon the trigger caught in the brush, and off it went.

On double quick we rushed the east side of Black Rock. Those on top gave us a volley, the bullets coming uncomfortably close. We returned the fire; one Indian dropped, the others fell back and hid in the crevices of their fort, high up in the air away from all harm. We could not ascend to its summit, nor could we dislodge them. Their position was a Gibraltar itself.

We had no repeating guns and were delayed in reloading.

Glenn, with several others, reserved their shots and broke ahead for camp. We followed to the rancheria, a large cave with numerous small ones close by. Here were the embers that created the column of smoke that led us on like a pillar of fire, but the residents of the dirty domicile had flown and left behind a few dirty rags, mortars, old baskets, fish and deer bones and prints of feet.

Firing was going on briskly on the opposite side of the stream, and they were speedily arrested in their flight up the deep ravine, north from the rock, by the captain's force, who were firing now incessantly on them. Our party ran to the creek, plunged in regardless of getting our clothes wet in regaining the north side, and quickly scrambled up the bank.

The first object that greeted us was a dead Indian lying on his back, shot through the breast; farther on one of the captain's party had two Indian children down — the agitation of his mind approaching distraction — for he had cut the throat of one and was about to repeat this diabolical and hellish act when several guns were leveled on him, and two of us wrenched the little Indian from his grasp.

We remonstrated with with him, told him he had done wrong in the sight of both God and man, and that we did not come to kill defenseless women and children nor to set an example for Indians to retaliate upon white families.

Firing by this time had ceased, with the exception of an Indian away up the south side of the canyon, who at regular intervals would elevate his gun and shoot. The balls would fall harmlessly to the earth and far from us.

The boy captured was called "Dick." His age was about 6 years; his dress consisted of an old smoky flour sack, with a hole cut in the bottom for his head, and holes in the sides for his arms, and had a large coil of glass beads encircling his neck. He was an apathetic little savage, possessed of the regular Indian stoicism; he uttered no word, nor did he shed a tear at the sight of the dead Indians as we led him around, viewing the corpses lying in the gulch.

Pity, though, was depicted on the faces of many of our comrades at the sight of an expiring Indian mother, her prattling babe by her side, unconscious of the horrible scenes enacted by ourselves.

James Payton, of Red Bluff, who composed one of the party on the north side, says that it was utterly impossible to distinguish a squaw from a buck when they came upon the bank of the dark gulch, and saw the Indians fleeing up its bed — for it was overshadowed by live oak and pepperwood trees — and that the killing of the squaw was unintentional and unavoidable.

Black Rock is about 400 feet in height, conical shaped, composed of what geologists term columnar basalt, and stands immediately on the south side of Mill Creek, which sweeps its base.

After reuniting our force of 16 we tramped down the canyon from the bloody and memorable place to Doctor Inskip's camp, where we found plenty provisions cooked and waiting for us.

A detachment, including Dr. Inskip, next day visited the battle ground and found that the Indians during the night had returned and buried their dead, all in one grave. The doctor claimed, from a certain sign on the mound, that it contained 17 bodies.

For several days following, detached portions of our force went skirmishing over the hills but found nothing further than, that the Indians had passed over the divide toward Deer Creek. Therefore we disbanded.

The company unanimously declared "Dick" my captive, whom I led by the hand to our home on Paynes Creek. Dick was received in my father's household with wonder, curiosity and kindness. Clothes were quickly converted to fit him, and the day following our arrival his appearance had much changed, but as yet, no utterance had escaped the lips of this dusky boy, who stuck to me wherever I went, from the day of his capture or rescue, and long after, we got home, where we were looked upon as Crusoe and Friday, but gradually our greatness wore away and ere long we were considered not above par with the other members of our family.

On the last day of March, 1860, we were endeavoring to corral a sow and pigs. The little Indian who had maintained the utmost silence, was laughing in great glee, when my sister, now Mrs. B.F. Thompson of Santa Clara, said, "Dick, what do you call them?"

"Cushew, Cushew," he answered, and from thence on we considered Richard was himself again.

During the two years stay with us he learned to converse moderately well, and we elicited considerable history of his tribe. Hi Good, Sandy Young and Bill Sublette made frequent raids upon this same tribe and killed great number.

From what this boy informed, us, I will now endeavor to explain the seeming indifference of the Indians on top of Black Rock at the time we were laying in wait for the captain's men to advance, and so very close to them. This tribe had heard of other Indians being moved (among which were Shave Head's band), to the Nome Lackee Reservation, and had concluded to go whenever the "Big man (General Kibbe) and his men" should come.

I suppose they knew of our coming from the time we departed the lake, as an Indian reconnoitered us at that point.

The men on top of the rock were the chiefs or big men of the tribe, including Dick's father. They were going to speak from that elevation to an Indian who would come with the big man's party. All the old men were up the canyon, in a cave, but would come out if all was right on our arrival.

And in our firing they found their mistake, which must also be admitted of our own; for according to his statement we could have cleared this canyon of the last Indian, (as they were all close by and willing to depart), by conducting them to Red Bluff where the government authorities would most certainly have taken them in charge and placed them on a reservation.

I have mentioned John Loree's death; he was killed at the Judd Ranch (now J.C. Turner's) in 1858, and when found, one arm had been severed from the body. Dick gave this revelation: The limb was brought to Black Rock and the entire tribe had a circular dance with Loree's arm in the center, and the Indians considered this a most powerful trophy.

Again he related that just before this, (which was one of the first murders in this section) two men named Maple and John, who had been living with the Indians, selecting wives from the squaws; and one day they got into an altercation regarding the women, when Maple killed John; shortly after the Indians dispatched Maple.

One of his most surprising revelations (to me at least) was that the dying woman with the child by her side was his mother.

Regarding their religious superstitions and laws he was too

young to be correctly impressed; however the "Big God" Indian of all was of preponderous dimensions; he could step from one ridge to another with all ease, and was much feared by all his tribe.

But the most common God was the bear, an animal, which they never killed. Dick related an incident consistent with this: His grandmother had been in a marsh digging roots, and in coming home a large bear reared up in front and disputed the passage with the old lady; but she gave him a whack with her Camas stick across the nose, when he departed.

After returning to the camp, she related the encounter, and the Indians were about to dispatch her; but just in the nick of time came Achetle, the Big God, who stood astride the canyon, and told the Indians to let her go, or he would cut off the salmon supply from Mill Creek, and drive all the deer from their country. He seemed to have some knowledge of family relations.

The Nosea Indians of Mill Creek, a once considerable tribe of people, have figured prominently in times past, but are daily becoming forgotten. No historical records mention them. Bancroft's History of Races of the Pacific States overlooked them.

There was in 1862 a small company of United States soldiers stationed for several months at Judd Ranch; during their stay here they purchased several head of cattle from D.G. Anderson. I am confident this detachment would have made it hot for any Indian to have come inside of Judd's enclosure. They never saw the home of the savage, nor had any longing desire to penetrate the rough canyons in quest of the enemy.

The redeemable feature of these regulars was this: They purchased Judd's hay crop as it stood on the stalk, which kept the soldiers in action daily, cutting the hay with their sabers and carrying it out to the big marsh ... [illegible].

... Now supposing Judd and Anderson had gone in with a big contractor (providing Judd's marsh would have been of sufficient area and Anderson had the required number of cattle, and the Indians whooped up at the proper time, to the necessary pitch), today they might be millionaires.

We have read the estimated cost of killing Indians, during the Modoc campaign at not less than $10,000 per head. Thereby the Inskip company in killing 17 Indians saved the United States

$170,000. Then we will include those killed by Rudolf Klotz's company, shortly after the massacre of Mrs. Dersch, those killed by Hi Good, Sandy Young, Bill Sublette and others. Place the total number at 100 Nosea, the government was saved of an expenditure of $1,000,000.

It is remarkable that the latter three named persons have died violent deaths and all poor. Maybe there are citizens who yet remember of a bounty fund once placed in the safe of Thomas Boarman for the scalps of these Indians, but for obvious good reasons the money was withdrawn. Perhaps Miel ... [illegible] ... Kennedy or Treasurer P.C. Scott recorded the circumstance.

Dick, the little Indian, lives in one of the lower counties, and has linked his fortune with a dusky maiden of Indian and Mexican parentage, is quite industrious for an Indian, an expert at shearing sheep, and makes a good citizen. He frequently sends us his best wishes through Mr. B.F. Thompson of Santa Clara.

He continues to claim to be a descendant of a once powerful tribe and considers himself the last of his race; however, he, as well as a number of settlers east of the Sacramento River, have been much mistaken by entertaining the latter idea, for during the latter part of last year we were all astonished at the appearance of several Indians among us who have maintained the greatest secrecy for nearly a score of years.

Different ones have appeared at different times at Mr. Turner's. To show what extreme caution coupled with fiendish desperation they resorted to, Mr. Turner says on the coming of two squaws with a boy to to his house they were much excited and showed by signs the oldest of the two had lost her child by one of the Indians braining the papoose with a rock, on account of its crying whilst they were trying to dodge around unperceived. These two squaws were taken to Red Bluff, and I believe they are now at Redding.

The few yet remaining are a poor, degraded and pitiful number of human beings, afraid of their shadows, and travel these rough hills like so many wild animals. They are wild in every sense, nor can they be easily approached. If so the considerate portion of this community would readily supply their wants, for it is much cheaper to feed and clothe them than to replenish our store after their very cunning thefts.

I would venture to say that the settlers living in Sierra township for the past twenty years have sustained losses to the amount of thousands of dollars by these Indians. I, myself, living in an isolated place, have been "wiped out" four different times in the last four years.

Though great good, in a manner, has resulted in finding out the perpetrators of the past mysterious robberies. Mr. Smith would come along and state that his house had been robbed, and he thought Jones did it. Jones also comes along and declares that he was cleaned out by those Smiths; he saw prints of naked feet for a distance, which would be lost in stepping upon the rocks, endeavoring to play Indian on him, "when every body knows there are none in the country."

They have eluded the keen eye of the hunter, save a couple of times, but their statements would be generally discredited.

Perhaps one of the most perplexing but rather amusing robberies by this little band, transpired last summer in the vicinity where I now write.

A prominent physician of Red Bluff accompanied me to look after some mining ground. After arriving in camps and examining the excavation close by, we put a pot of beans over the fire, which cooked during the night. Next morning at breakfast we merely sampled them, and put in an additional seasoning prior to our going up on the ridge to look at the shaft and tunnel, placing the beans on the fire to simmer until our return.

The entire number three of us, left to make the required examination by panning earth and carrying the same some distance to water. The sun had passed the meridian ere we started for our dinner. We found ourselves hungry; the doctor remarked he was eager to get back to the pot of beans, "for they were just splendid."

We mounted our animals and rode to camp, which consisted of a tent and a brush arbor — tent for sleeping and arbor for cooking. But on nearing we saw our kitchen badly demoralized: our entire larder had disappeared — bacon, flour, sugar, coffee, rice, etc., along with that most coveted pot of beans, pot and all. The tent had been relieved of our clothing, bedding, eight trade dollars, and the doctor's leather wallet containing his medicines.

We, however, were a temperate trio; we looked serious and doleful for a moment, when the doctor remarked with a smile, "I guess they have not got that bottle of whisky that I brought along as an antidote for snake bites and hid in this cluster of poison oak," drawing it forth, "for the contortions of death in starvation are equally as horrifying as that caused by snake bites, and spirit stimulants are administered in both cases. Let us take a drink, and hasten for the settlements."

J.D. Potts, president of a mining company which I am connected with, at the time the Indians visited Turner's, instructed me to purchase, at the company's expense, provisions and have them conveyed thither to feed those there, and induce others to come in. Unfortunately this philanthropic design was frustrated; in time several inexperienced parties found their camp — not by any prowess displayed on their part — for an Indian let them.

After which the incendiary torch was applied by these brave white men, destroying the winter stores of those remaining out, and showing an example of treachery to their Indian pilot, who was endeavoring to get his wild and untutored brothers to quit their savage life and adopt that of civilization.

While here they also exhausted their ammunition in making the hills resound, cannonading the rocks and other objects, for they saw no Indians, after which they returned home all covered with glory.

Rod D. McDonald deserves much praise, for prior to the above strategic move toward getting the Indians in, he along and without arms accompanied by the Indian boy, spoken of, to the rancheria, made an examination of the camp and returned unharmed.

I will give, in brief, an incident relating to D.B. Lyons, present superintendent of the Sierra Lumber Company, and the Indians at the time of locating the Tehama County wagon road, he being one of the viewers. When nearing Battle Creek Meadows Mr. Lyon received a message to return to Red Bluff on business for Wells, Fargo & Co.

Unaccompanied he traversed the old Dye mill road, and on nearing Coyote Springs he discovered a number of Indians coming toward him loaded with beef, as they had just killed an animal close by. Several dropped their loads and fired volley upon volley at the lone horseman, who spurred on his horse, by which he made extraordinary time in getting to Red Bluff.

What material for history! Were it only hunted up and put in the hands of a competent chronicler, information of the Nosea tribe of Indians, Mill Creek, Tehama County, California, would be more thrilling and entertaining, and far more sympathetic, than the history of their neighbors — the Modocs — especially the little remnant yet among us.

What great changes have been wrought in this township since our first adventure on Mill Creek after Indians. Numerous large sawmills have been built, miles of flume constructed to convey lumber to the valley, and a railroad in operation for a distance of nine miles with a locomotive that hauls lumber from the Yellow Jacket to the Champion Mill, from whence it is dumped into the flume.

School houses stand on many ridges, well-improved farms are found in places which in those days were inhabited by Indians and wild animals. Such is the progress of the western slope of the Sierras in our county, which keeps pace with the go-ahead spirit of the great American people.

Of Dr. Inskip: He was a good and intelligent neighbor, possessed of great natural shrewdness, invincible energy and perseverance. It is hardly possible that one who endured so many hardships through life, for the public good, should be so soon forgotten. In glancing through the lately published tinsel *History of Tehama County,* I could not discover his name; it was wholly omitted.

Dr. Inskip, who was a Nestor among pioneers of this state, as also of Idaho where, upon Jordan Creek, he was besieged for days by hostile Bannocks, his house literally riddled by bullets and several of his companions killed before succor came, now sleeps beneath the shadow of the dark butte which bears his name.

This noted landmark, with its most wonderful cave, is discernible from Red Bluff by looking north of east and over the Tuscan Buttes. In the past ten years a diversity of names have been applied to the butte -- Anderson, Soap, Hickman, White, etc.

In conclusion, and as the humble author of this disjointed and poorly written article, I do most solemnly offer my earnest protest against any other name superseding that of Inskip, applied to the butte; and may posterity forever carry the name of Inskip down the corridor of time in connection with this, one of the picturesque butte which helps for the poetic and grand chain of the Sierras, presenting a beautiful view to the city of Red Bluff.

ADDENDA

On the 16th of last month, whilst the residents of Buck's Flat were partaking of their noonday meal, they were startled by the appearance of four Indians coming to the place — one very old man and a quite aged squaw; these two persons were all of 80 years of age; the others a man of 40 and a boy of 10 years of age. They walked in with hands extended upward, thereby declaring friendly manifestations.

The aged man handed Mr. Boles $24.75 in coin, consisting of one $20 gold piece dated 1874, nine half-dollar pieces, their dates ranging from 1858 to 1879, the twenty-five cent piece worn smooth.

They were given provisions and a place was assigned for them to camp within the yard and by the smoke house. They appeared very submissive, and would not leave the campfire without consulting some one of the family.

On the afternoon of their arrival Mr. Boles started off to apprise Mr. Jacob Turner of the presence of the Indians. This was another poorly conceived idea, for his movements were watched by the keen eyes of the Indians with much distrust. Afterward Mr. J.W. Hamilton came riding to the ranch from the Yellow Jacket sawmill, stayed but a short time then departed. This also seemed to cause much uneasiness among the Indians, who did not go to bed, but remained squatted around the fire until Mr. Avery and family retired. When he woke in the morning he found the Indians had fled.

Mr. Avery says they were a hard-looking lot of American citizens and seemed to be in mourning for the dead. The two aged ones had what appeared to be a skull cap made of clay. They would try to give an explanation of the death of two children.

Mr. Avery said they took great interest in examining the old relics that had been collected from the ranch, consisting of stone platters, mortars, pestles, etc., which seemed to amuse them much, and, perhaps, called for the recollections of bygone days when they were members of a once numerous race, now dwindled down to themselves.

Chapter 9

Monument marking the site of the Nome Lackee Indian Reservation near Paskenta, in western Tehama County. It's unclear if the monument is still there. If it is, it's behind a locked gate.

'The Indian Problem'

Following the 1860 attack on the Yahi at Black Rock, there was a period of peace in the relations between the natives and the settlers on the east side of the Sacramento Valley. There are neither accounts of serious Indian depredations, nor of the bloody raids of retribution that invariably followed.

The reason is obvious: There were only a few small free

California Indian bands left that could have come into conflict with the newcomers. Such bands did exist — Yahi history was not unique in the years after the Gold Rush — but those marginalized bands had been taught, with viciousness, that if it came to violence, the newcomers were far better at it.

In light of that, it's almost curious that the pattern of bloodshed would resume in 1862 around the valley. But the new pattern of conflict was different, and appears to have been rooted in California's solution to "The Indian Problem," and how that solution changed with the coming of the Civil War.

The Indian Problem is that the people who were in North America first were in the way of those who followed. Genocide was the initial solution undertaken, but killing off whole tribes fell out of favor as there was a less distasteful option: Just push the first peoples farther west. Relocation to Oklahoma and elsewhere became national default policy. There were many more than one "Trail of Tears" in the 1830s and the years that followed.

But in California, pushing the natives west just wouldn't work because there was an ocean in the way. There were actually proposals to move the California Indians to Hawaii or the islands off the Southern California coast. An eastward option was aired that would have pushed the tribes into the Great Basin of Nevada and Utah. None of those options were feasible and they got little serious consideration.

A new concept emerged, which involved setting aside areas within California — reserving them — for the people who had the indisputable primary claim to the land. That would open up the rest of the state to the newcomers, perhaps without conflict.

So in 1851 and 1852, a party of federal commissioners traveled up and down the state, negotiating 18 treaties with 139 separate Indian bands. The contracts set aside 7.5 million acres for California's natives, a bit more than 7 percent of the state's total land.

The sanctuaries laid out by commissioners — Redick McKee, George W. Barbour, and O.M. Wozencraft — were designed to get the Indians off what appeared to be the most economically valuable lands for the newcomers.

The big reservation planned in the Sacramento Valley, for instance, swept across 227 square miles of Butte County from

John Bidwell's and Sam Neal's properties around Chico and Durham, southeast to Oroville and the Big Bend of the Feather River near Yankee Hill. It reached up into the foothills to encompass present-day Paradise, but not as high as Magalia. Nine tribes signed on to that treaty.

Those reserved lands in their native state are largely grasslands on the valley floor, and blue oak and gray pine woodlands in the foothills, all with shallow soil over a layer of hardened volcanic mudflow. On their face, they aren't prime lands.

But the reservation included the gold fields that would later be developed in Butte Creek Canyon, and the fabulous treasures of Cherokee, where millions of dollars in gold were found, as well as the only diamonds ever mined in California.

Those prizes were discovered between the conclusion of the negotiations and the time when the 18 treaties came up before Congress for ratification. By then, similar discoveries occurred up and down the state. So the California congressional delegation saw to it that the treaties were not ratified. Not only that, the agreements were hidden away so deep that even the memory of them was lost for decades.

The California solution

But California's Indian Problem did not go away. The state had the densest native population in North America prior to contact with the Europeans, with a population of perhaps as many as half a million people, although a figure around 300,000 seems to be the most accepted now.

Most of them died from introduced diseases. California natives had no immunities to the ailments brought by the newcomers, and each new introduced strain felled hundreds and thousands of the first peoples.

The process had begun at the missions, where 60-80 percent of those gathered in by the padres perished. That was followed by the malaria brought by the Hudson Bay trappers in the 1830s that killed a third to a half of the Indians in the Central Valley. The Gold Rush brought a new wave of killer diseases, including venereal disease, which took a devastating toll when it was introduced into native communities.

A large number of the natives were simply killed by the newcomers, but wanton killing couldn't be government policy, and some Indians survived the new diseases and passed on resistance to the ailments to their young. It's estimated about 60,000 natives survived in 1860, still enough to be a problem for the newcomers.

The solution that evolved for California was two-pronged, although it didn't happen by plan. Quite independently, both the state and federal government came up with their own solutions.

Sacramento passed laws allowing the enslavement of the Indians to the settlers. Washington approved a system of collecting and confining those who remained free to what we would today call concentration camps.

The state acted first, with the Indian Government and Protection Act of 1850. It nominally was drafted to prevent the exploitation of the native people, but then actually set out several ways to do just that.

Slavery of Indian children was allowed under the guise of "apprenticeship," a simple procedure conducted by a justice of peace. The children could be held until they were considered adults. That was originally age 18 for boys and 15 for girls, but that was later amended to as high as 30 and 25 years, respectively.

In addition, adult Indians identified by any settler as idle or vagrant could also be arrested, with their labor auctioned off to the highest bidder.

As a result, nearly every ranch of any size had numerous Indian laborers. Even many simple urban households had one or more Indian domestic workers. Native concubines and wives were also obtained this way, to compensate for the fact far fewer women than men came west in the Gold Rush.

Abuse is not a given in these cases. A fair number of Indian women taken as sexual partners were treated as wives in the best sense of the word. Many domestic workers were treated like part of the family they worked for. Many Indian laborers were paid for their work. But there was exploitation, and even in the best cases, the natives didn't have the choice.

The federal part of the solution had been formally proposed in 1852 by California Superintendent of Indians Edward Fitzgerald

Beale. He recognized that separating Indians from the onslaught of Western civilization was their best chance for survival. He suggested creating a series of large military posts to which the Indians would be gathered and protected. They wouldn't be forts as much as a modern version of the old Spanish missions. Or at least, of the rosy romanticized myth the missions had become in those days. It's a myth believed even up to the present to a degree.

The missions were believed to have thrived on Indian labor, with a limited amount of outside investment. The common view was that the Indians had been taught Christian values and learned valuable skills. They had supported themselves in a manner that didn't grate on European sensitivities.

That was exactly what the settlers of the 1850s were looking for: A place to stick Indians, where they'd take care of themselves and learn to be proper white folk. And the idea that the reservations could be self-sufficient after a small initial investment was attractive to Congress.

So in March 1852, Congress approved five reservations of up to 25,000 acres in California.

The first was created the following year at Fort Tejon in Southern California.

At that point Beale was forced out of office. He is reported to have a true compassion for the California Indians. That led him to ignore the balky bureaucratic chain of command stretching back to Washington, in favor of getting things done in a timely manner. That was not politically wise, as he was bypassing officials appointed by congressmen and senators through the spoils system in place at the time.

Beale was replaced by Thomas J. Henley. A three-term congressman from Indiana prior to coming to California, he understood how the government worked. Unfortunately he also seems to have understood that money could be made in the position he held. He was the wrong man for the job at its critical juncture, and that crippled the project's success.

Henley was able to establish the other four authorized reservations. His first was Nome Lackee, up against the coast ranges in western Tehama County, created in September 1854.

The reservation was named for the resident Indians. It

encompassed a rough triangle that stretched from Thomes Creek north to Elder Creek, and included what are now the towns of Paskenta and Flournoy.

It is this reservation and the Mendocino Reservation, created in 1856 on the California North Coast at present day Fort Bragg, that we are most interested in, as they are relevant to our story.

Nome Lackee was created to take in the Indians from the Sacramento Valley and the surrounding foothills, but it was too close to the natives' homelands. When things turned bad on the reservation, the occupants would just walk away and head home.

The Yuba Indians were famous for this. They'd been able to earn good wages laboring in the gold fields along the river system in Yuba, Nevada and Sierra counties that bore their name. They'd been taken to Nome Lackee in June 1857, and the first of many escapes and recaptures was reported by the *Red Bluff Beacon* less than a month later.

The Mendocino Reservation became the preferred alternative for Central Valley as it was more remote. However, the climate there — foggy, wet and cold — was foreign and unhealthy to natives from interior California. It's not prime farming country, which meant it needed to be more heavily supported, a challenge due to its remote location.

The supply problem is why a search was launched for an easier land route to the Mendocino Reservation. The search stumbled onto Round Valley in the midst of the coast ranges, about halfway between Fort Bragg and Nome Lackee.

The valley, around the current town of Covelo, was by most accounts perfect. It was remote enough that Indians wouldn't just wander away. There were few neighboring communities of settlers. It was fertile and temperate; sufficient for crops without the chill of the coast or the oven of the interior. The Indians living in the area were friendly, not opposed to hosting other natives.

But it may have been too perfect. In the two years it took to establish the Nome Cult Farm there, the southern half of the valley was occupied by white settlers, who moved in with such a heavy hand that they antagonized the original residents. Indian children were kidnapped to work on the new farms, and resistance was met with murder. The people who settled there seemed to have been unusually cruel. By the time the new reservation was established, the valley was embroiled in conflict between the natives and the newcomers.

Corruption and incompetence

The accounts available in the first few years after the reservations were created describe a glowing success almost immediately. The official reports indicated there were thousands of safe, happy, industrious Indians at the reservations. They were building proper houses, plowing hundreds of acres to raise grain and maintaining gardens producing abundant produce.

Accounts in local newspapers agreed, and tours by leading citizens of the communities around the reservations offered glowing endorsements of the system's success. It's an open question whether the locals did in fact find marvelous facilities or were willing to fudge the truth in order to keep the Indians out of the way, which was their ultimate objective.

There were contrary reports, often from the officers leading the federal military attachments attached to each reservation to provide security. It's likely these just moved up the military chain of command and got little notice from the public or civilian policy-makers.

There was, however, a federal investigator in the state who was making more serious allegations against the Henley administration. It's not exactly clear what government agency J. Ross Browne was working for, but his reports of fraud and mistreatment of Indians on the reservations were echoed by the Alta California newspaper in 1858.

Special Agent G. Bailey was sent to California to look into the claims, and found them to largely be true. Vincent Geiger, who ran the Nome Lackee reservation, was singled out. He was accused for jiggering a survey of the reservation in such a way that prime lands were left out. Those lands were then claimed by Geiger and the Titus brothers, also employees of the reservation.

Geiger and the Tituses "apprenticed" dozens of Indians sent to be cared for on the reservation instead to work the purloined lands, as well diverting to their use equipment and resources the government purchased for the reservation.

The pattern was repeated at Nome Cult and Mendocino. Many of those who'd claimed much of Round Valley were family members or business associates of reservation employees up to and including Superintendent Henley. At the Mendocino Reservation, a private sawmill had been established on reservation lands.

Bailey called the Mendocino Reservation a total failure, and wrote Nome Lackee barely fed and clothed the Indians there. There were no signs of a dozen frame houses reportedly built at Nome Lackee for the Indians, and they were living instead in traditional native structures.

But there weren't many Indians at Nome Lackee. The place was largely deserted. Geiger claimed there had been a crop failure and the Indians had left, and he didn't have the manpower to bring them back. It's more likely he just didn't care. Fewer Indians took less of his time, and allowed more of the rations and equipment sent to the reservations to be used for his and his associates' private ventures

Bailey suggested abandoning Nome Lackee and Mendocino in favor of Nome Cult. It would take a few years to accomplish that officially, but by the early 1860s there were effectively no Indians on the first two sites, except those attached to households of white families living on the land.

Recognizing Browne and Bailey had created a problem for him, Henley resigned shortly after their reports came out. Being politically connected, he landed on his feet as postmaster of San Francisco.

Geiger had fewer patrons. He was fired in 1860. He stayed in Tehama County, pursuing what appear to have been unsuccessful business ventures. He ended up stabbing a man to death in a barroom brawl in Red Bluff in September 1863, and then fled to Canada and later Chile, where he ultimately died.

Though most of Geiger's troubles appear to be of his own making, the job of running the Nome Lackee Reservation does appear to have been star-crossed.

The first supervisor, Henry Lewis Ford, died July 2, 1860, in a freak accident while mounting a horse. A pistol hanging on the saddle pommel discharged and hit him in the neck, killing him instantly.

His successor, Edward A. Stevenson, moved to a ranch across the river from Red Bluff after his term on the reservation. That is the house that was burned in May 1859 by an Indian servant, killing seven people, including Stevenson's wife and children. That incident is recounted in Chapter 7.

The tripod

The civilian federal authorities charged with the welfare of the native peoples were just one of three government authorities working to get the California Indians out of the way of the onslaught of Western Civilization.

The other two legs of the tripod were military, and it's widely misunderstood that there were two separate official military forces in 1860.

Both the federal and state governments had their own independent military authority then. This is a point that often causes confusion today. We read a reference to "soldiers" from that period and assume a single chain of command, stretching to Washington.

That wasn't the case in 1860. Most of the armed men operating under government authority in that era in the United States answered to their governor rather than the president.

It's a concept foreign to us today, as the state militias have been replaced by the National Guard. Parts of the Guard can still be called to action by a governor to address an emergency caused by storm, earthquake or even domestic unrest. But the idea a governor could mount a military offensive against some of the residents of his state is incomprehensible today.

Not so then. The 1859 campaign of California Adjutant General William Kibbe is recounted earlier in this book. The state also authorized bands of "rangers" in that era to root out the Indians in several other locales. Indeed the Indians gathered up by Kibbe in Northeastern California were sent to the already-failing Mendocino Reservation initially rather than Nome Cult because another state-authorized band operating under the command of Walter Jarboe was on the rampage in the vicinity of Nome Cult at the time.

His "Eel River Rangers" raged from July 1859 to January 1860, when their actions had become so egregious that Gov. John Weller disbanded them. In his official report, Jarboe claimed they had killed 283 Indians, a number that federal military authorities suggested was low by about half.

Almost any time you read of outrages committed by soldiers in this era, you are reading about the actions of state troops rather than the federal regulars. The state of California viewed its original inhabitants as obstacles and nothing more. It wanted the natives out of the way and had the authority to use gunpowder to pursue that goal.

The federal military, on the other hand, was a remarkably professional organization for that era, matching up well with any national force worldwide. Many if not most of its officers, even down to the most junior grades, were graduates of West Point. Their training instilled a sense of responsibility to the Constitution's protection of human rights, even if many in California regarded the native population as less than human.

Again and again the regulars were called in to protect the settlers from Indian depredations, and again and again upon arrival on the scene they discovered that it was the Indians who needed the protection more than the settlers. A case in point is recounted in chapter 7 of this book.

It would have been easier for the federal troops to ride the wind of public opinion and take on the extermination the locals sought. But the regulars did not do that.

This, again, is a difficult concept for us to understand today. Our view of the federal military's interaction with the native peoples is colored by the warfare on the Great Plains following the Civil War. By then the feds had bought into the extermination idea. But Custer never came to California. When it came down to killing Indians, California did it without Washington's help.

1861

The tripod, with all its flaws, was at least stable.

One leg was a civilian authority filled with people who regarded the Indians as an asset to be exploited rather than nurtured. Even the most callous of government officials recognized their culpability if they ignored their job completely, but almost none of them put much effort into doing it well.

Then there was the state with its military, which wanted the Indians out of the way. That was counterbalanced by the federal military, which in those days didn't distinguish between white and Indian when determining which Americans to protect.

But it all collapsed in 1861, and Indian troubles in the Sacramento Valley resumed shortly thereafter.

By then, Nome Lackee and Mendocino were pretty well abandoned. The Indians at those sites had been collected at Nome Cult, but it wasn't secure. The neighbors to the reservation had the habit of running their cattle into the Indian grain fields to feed, and punishing to the point of murder any native who resisted. Leaving the reservation was also treated as a capital crime by the settlers around it.

There was even competition for the acorn crop, which the settlers used as hog feed.

The year had started badly for the Nome Cult Indians, with a severe winter that pushed them to the edge of starvation. With no alternative, they raided neighboring farms, prompting attacks of retribution. A "recent fight" reported Jan. 30 in the *Red Bluff Beacon* — the account drawn from the *Mendocino Herald* — said 18 Indians were killed in that single incident. It was not the only report of conflict that year.

But the real problem dates to April 1861, thousands of miles away, when the newly seceded Confederate state of South Carolina opened fire on Fort Sumter in Charleston harbor, and the Civil War was on.

Within a few months, all the regular army troops in California, save a few batteries of cannons protecting San Francisco Bay, were recalled to the East Coast.

The California Indians' only true protector was gone. Their place was taken by California volunteer units. They were under federal command, but many had the mindset of the state troops like Jarboe's rangers, that the Indians were something less than human, and in the way. And the professional officers who had led the regulars were gone as well, many of them gone from wearing lieutenant's and captain's bars to general's stars in both the Union and Confederate armies.

The California Indians were in the care of armed men who wanted them gone, and civilian authorities who really didn't give a damn. It's hard to fault the natives for trying, one last doomed time, to take their fate into their own hands.

Chapter 10

The author views Mill Creek Canyon in this photo taken by his wife in the 1990s. Much of the canyon was empty after the decimation of the Yahi in the 1850s and 1860, and its ruggedness provided sanctuary for California natives rebelling against the reservation system and the newcomers in general. The renegades became the dreaded "Mill Creeks," and their actions were mistakenly attributed to the Yahi.

The Yahi are not the 'Mill Creeks'

The five years beginning in 1862 saw a resumption of the bloodshed between the natives and the newcomers in the Sacramento Valley. It's sometimes called the Mill Creek War, as the violence on the Indian side was attributed to the Mill Creek Indians.

When later historians began trying to re-create the history of Ishi and by extension of the Yahi, they assumed the Mill Creeks of the 1860s were the Yahi. Mill Creek was Yahi country, and the tribe had raided settlers in the decade before.

But the raids of the 1860s were different from those of the 1850s. In the 1850s, the Yahi raided for food. In the 1860s, the raids seemed to be about vengeance. Women and/or children were killed each year, something all but unheard of in the 1850s.

In the 1860s, spoils of survival seemed to be an afterthought, and the kind of loot that was taken wasn't food, but rather things like coin and gold, fine fabrics and other niceties that wouldn't help keep an Indian alive up in the hills. They had value only to Indians who'd been engaged with the civilization that had taken over California.

What appears to have happened is that the term "Mill Creeks" took on a meaning equivalent to "boogeyman" in today's jargon. The Yahi had earned a bad reputation in the 1850s, and when the violence resumed in the 1860s, blaming it on the Mill Creeks shortened the learning curve.

And there's a geographical reason as well: Some of the Indian raiders took shelter in Yahi country, including cases where they where actually pursued to the banks of Mill Creek. It was still the land no one else wanted, a harsh and hostile sanctuary against the civilization of the day. And it was largely empty due to the damage inflicted on the Yahi.

By 1862, there wouldn't have been a lot of Yahi left. The grinding warfare of the late-1850s and the attack at Black Rock in 1860 had likely reduced them to a small enough group that it could survive in the resources of a homeland shrunken to its core.

I envision the Yahi at this time as a single village of 50 to 100 people, hunkered down on Mill Creek a few miles upstream from Black Rock, a place most isolated from their neighbors. They appear to have still been traveled to the high meadows in summer — or at least some of them did — as Ishi was familiar with the seasonal migration. Maintaining a group even as small as 50 people would have required some movement to utilize the resources of survival, as those resources shifted with the calendar.

But the high meadows were then being settled by the newcomers. Richard Morgan had come to Morgan Valley in the early 1850s, according to the Tehama County Genealogical and Historical Society's 2007 history of the county. The Rawson brothers were running sheep in Battle Creek Meadows by 1860, according to the same book, and the unfortunate Kendall Bumpass was settled there in 1862.

That was three years before Bumpass would take the editor of the *Red Bluff Sentinel* newspaper up to what is now Lassen Volcanic National Park to show him a geothermal feature now known as Bumpass Hell. During the tour Bumpass broke through a thin crust over a mass of pyroclastic water and scorched a leg to the point it had to be cut off, after an agonizing trip back to Red Bluff.

It was an era when wagon roads were being driven across the mountains from Redding, Red Bluff and Chico to Susanville. The Tehama County Wagon Road in particular ran right through the Yahi summer homeland, paralleling modern day Highway 36 through Battle Creek Meadows, Morgan Valley and Childs Meadow, before turning east to Wilson Lake and modern day Chester.

For the Yahi to have traveled and lived for a season in this relatively bustling remoteness would have required stealth, caution — and the complicity of the newcomers.

That complicity isn't to suggest a formal pact or agreement, or even any communication. Rather it would have been a recognition by the Indians that the white folk became homicidal if their animals and other stuff was messed with, and an uncertainty on the part of the whites as to exactly how many Indians were out there. There's little doubt the whites in the high meadows knew they weren't alone. But the handful of settlers didn't know how much company they had.

It was, I believe, a situation where fear produced discretion on both sides. The Yahi stayed out of sight as best they could, and pursued deer rather than the sheep of the first herds brought to the high country. The whites busied themselves with chores other than killing Indians for no particular reason.

I volunteered a few years back for a couple of archaeological digs with the Lassen National Forest in the upper meadows, and spent much of a week on a site a hundred yards or so up a slope, in a location that at first glance didn't seem a likely spot. It ended up being quite rich in artifacts. It seemed to have been picked to be out of sight, but still close to the resources that had once sustained a large village the meadow below, evidenced by a huge mound.

You could picture a small hunting party camped there on the slope, some perhaps remembering wistfully a summer when the meadow would have been full of Yahi. There weren't enough of them left to crowd the meadow anymore, and the smoke rising from a settler's compound a half-mile farther on would have made it clear those days were gone.

The Yahi's existence had always been tenuous, but never as much as in the 1860s. Ranchers worked the lower Yahi foothills, and logging operations occupied the Antelope Creek drainage and towered over Deer Creek from the Cohasset ridge. The summer larder of the high meadows was only available to small, furtive hunting parties. Finding enough food to survive would have been an all-encompassing task.

But from 1862 to 1866, the Mill Creeks were blamed for raids stretching from the vicinity of current day Lake Oroville to Shasta Lake, a stretch of about 100 miles. It simply doesn't make sense for the raiders to be the Yahi. There weren't enough of them to take on those kinds of crusades.

Many of the "Mill Creeks" of the 1860s spoke English, which the isolationist Yahi never had the opportunity to master. The raiders' weapons of choice were firearms, which don't seem to have become common among the Yahi, and at some point appear to have been abandoned altogether in favor of the quieter bow and arrow that suited the life of hiding the tribe was forced to adopt.

Instead, the new Mill Creeks were probably escapees from the Nome Cult Farm. They bolted from the reservation, embittered by the abuse of its neighbors, the inability of the military to protect them, and the disinterest, incompetence and corruption of the civilian authorities. They appear to have been collections of malcontents — and justifiably so — from several tribes.

The record of 1862 actually says as much.

Chapter 11

The ruins of Keefer's Mill, off Rock Creek north of Chico. In June 1862, residents of the area gathered here for protection after Indians killed a teamster and two teenage girls in the vicinity. The girls' younger brother was abducted, and his body was reportedly found elsewhere.

1862

Indians who were gathered on the Northern California reservations had a habit of leaving, but in 1862, the flight from Nome Cult reached a new level.

A raiding party hit the western Sacramento Valley in April, and a second was active in the foothills on the east side of the valley by June. Then in September, facing an ultimatum from their neighbors at Nome Cult, hundreds of the reservation residents left en masse to return to their Butte County homelands.

Three white children were killed by the group that appeared in the foothills of eastern Butte and Tehama counties in June, which triggered the elevated outrage and bloody retaliation that always followed the killing of women and children.

The violence in Butte and eastern Tehama counties was blamed on the Mill Creeks, but the settlers did not make the mistake of more modern anthropologists that their foes were Yahi. The people of the time recognized they were fighting renegades from the reservation, perhaps supplemented by local talent.

Some of those locals may have been Yahi, but the bulk of the tribe was continuing and refining the hidden isolation that had begun after the Black Rock attack in 1860. The tribe was likely missed by the bloodshed of 1862.

Eagle Peak

The first account of Indian troubles in the Sacramento Valley in 1862 is laid with little doubt on reservation renegades. It was a raid by about 30 Indians that began in April along the western edge of the valley.

It may have begun near Clear Lake, but when it got up into what's now western Glenn County late in April, two people were killed and a treasured horse was stolen. That's when a pursuit was mounted. It came to a head with a battle May 4 on the slopes of a promontory called Eagle Peak in western Tehama County, in which both Indians and settlers were killed.

The incident is little known today outside historians in its immediate neighborhood. The best source for information is the twice-a-year publication *Wagon Wheels*, of the Colusi County Historical Society, which has had several articles on the matter dating to 1954. The most recent ones, by Charles A. Martin, appear in the Fall 2000 and Spring 2011 editions.

The story begins with a band forming of Pit River and Hat Creek Indians from the reservation, and Cache Creek Wintuns from farther south, merging under the leadership of Hat Creek Lize.

Lize, said to be an unusually cruel woman of large stature, and an excellent shot with a gun or bow, had been gathered up by Adjutant General William Kibbe's campaign in 1859.

The raiders moved south toward Clear Lake before heading north up Stony Creek. They killed and butchered a prized racehorse near present-day Stonyford. Then on Grindstone Creek they came upon a Mr. Watson (whose first name appears alternately as Henry, Harry and Hiram) and a 12-year-old boy employed as a sheepherder. Both were killed and the raiders continued moving north.

The killing of the horse and Watson riled up the neighbors, though the boy is only mentioned in passing, which might suggest he was an Indian "apprentice."

A band of about 30 formed to pursue the Indian raiders, led by tracker "Big Jim," a "friendly Wintun Indian," according to a report by Gene Russell accompanying Martin's 2011 article.

The accounts indicate Hat Creek Lize's group didn't feel any particular concern about a pursuit, as they killed an oxen and took the time to hang and dry it at a camp on the southeastern slopes of Eagle Peak, a half-dozen miles northwest of Paskenta. Big Jim found them there and reported back to the posse.

The posse closed on their target, and camped for the night at an abandoned cabin in an area called the Goat Range. With the morning of May 4, 1862, they divided into two forces and moved forward, one climbing to get above the Indian camp and the other approaching from the east. They attacked at daybreak.

Both sides of the fight were roughly equal in numbers, but the superior weaponry of the settlers won the day. About 15 Indians were killed and a woman and child were captured. A newspaper account May 23 in Ukiah's *Mendocino Journal* claimed the prisoners were recognized as Indians from Nome Cult.

One white man, Thomas Shannon, was killed during the fight by an arrow to the heart and was buried at the scene. Two others were wounded and were carried back to Newville, in the vicinity of present-day Black Butte Reservoir. One, S.R. Ford, succumbed to his wounds but the other recovered.

The dead Indians were left where they fell, and their bones could be seen there a decade later, according to Martin's sources.

In Martin's account he repeats a story told by the daughter of raid participant Bernie Millsaps, who told her accurate arrow fire from an area of high grass pinned down several of the settlers at the height of the battle. The source of the arrows was located, rifle fire was directed at it, and the arrows ceased.

At the conclusion of the battle the dead archer was found to be a woman, perhaps Hat Creek Lize. She does appear later in the narrative of this year, but it may be that every large, aggressive Indian woman of that area was called Lize, just as every raiding party was called Mill Creeks.

In its earliest versions the story has a flourish that's too good to be true. The night before the attack, a card game — Pedro — was played, with the stakes being a coffin and a burial shroud. The winners were said to be Shannon and Ford, the men killed in the fight.

Martin recounts a much more believable version, that the game was played to determine which group of raiders would get the more dangerous approach to the camp. The two teams, with the macabre humor likely before a battle, were called the coffins and shrouds.

Trouble across the valley

By the following month, trouble had crossed to the east side of the Sacramento Valley in Butte and Tehama counties, and the accounts support the idea the Indians involved came from Nome Cult.

The *Butte Record* reported that on June 18 a meeting was held at Forks of Butte, the most upstream of the four mining towns in Butte Creek Canyon, to address Indian "depredations." The vigilante indictment cited the murders of Michael Walsh of Chico; "Mr. Dunbar or Dunlap" of Rock Creek, just north of Chico; and Mr. Haynes at Chico Meadows, where Big Chico Creek runs close to Butte Creek farther upstream, in the vicinity of current-day Butte Meadows. The Boy Scouts' Camp Lassen is located today in Chico Meadows.

Already there had been conflict, the *Record* reported, with what were identified as the Deer and Mill Creek Indians. A party had pursued, an Indian had been killed, and revenge against the whites was threatened.

That threat prompted the miners to bind together to defend themselves and assemble a force to attack the threatening force, said to consist of a hundred warriors drawn from four tribes.

The "hundred warriors" number sounds like the hyperbole typical from the Indian hunters of the era headed out to attack the "heathens," making their effort more heroic by inflating their foe. Really it's impossible to imagine where so many armed Indians could have come from.

But the idea that a hostile force drawn from four tribes had formed in the foothills of Butte and Tehama counties is quite reasonable. The caldron that could have forged such a mix was the Nome Cult reservation, just as it had forged the band attributed to Hat Creek Lize.

The incidents cited in the June 18 meeting happened in areas from which Kibbe's men had removed people in 1859, who ended up at Nome Cult. People disenchanted with the reservation could be expected to return to their homelands. They would find them dramatically altered and occupied by newcomers, who now regarded the the land as theirs and considered the original residents trespassers. That could only elevate the natives' ire. Violence was likely, as was retribution.

So it was that a party of 24 men was formed in late June at Forks of Butte to pursue the Indian renegades. The success of their campaign is unreported, because the Indians struck first in a raid that eclipsed interest in any effort the Butte Creek men might have mounted.

The Hickok children

As the settlers' expedition headed into the hills, a party of Indians appeared on the Cohasset Ridge. They may well have come from the northeast, moving to avoid the Butte Creek men. On June 25, they came upon teamster Thomas Allen, who was carrying a load of lumber from Morrill's sawmill on the ridge down the road to the valley floor. He was killed horribly, shot with more than a dozen arrows. His throat was cut and he was scalped, and his mules were also slaughtered.

However, an Indian boy with Allen escaped, although he was wounded. Indian Tom, who'd been taken in by the Keefers a few years earlier after a massacre in Deer Creek canyon, made his way to his employer's ranch at the foot of the hill and raised the alarm.

Women and children from the neighborhood were gathered at Keefer's Mill, and a party of armed men headed after the Indians.

They didn't find the raiders, but found Allen.

They also found the slain horses of the three Hickok children, who'd been gathering berries about a mile upstream from Keefer's Mill.

Scraps of clothing, torn off in the hasty flight through the brush, led searchers the next morning to the bodies of the

Monument in the Chico Cemetery marks the Hickok family plot. The names and ages of the three children killed in 1862 are engraved into its base.

two girls: Minnie and Ida. Their family headstone in the Chico Cemetery states Minnie S. Hickok was 13 years, 6 months and 7 days old at the time or her death. Ida A. Hickok was 16 years, 7 months and 9 days old.

The older girl was found nude, in a hole left by the roots of an uprooted tree, pierced by 30 arrows. The younger girl was found in a creek a bit downstream, fully dressed and shot with three arrows. There are differing reports whether the bodies were scalped or mutilated.

The boy Franklin, just under 7 years old, was still missing.

The incident inflamed the countryside. White war parties scoured the nearby hills with much anger, no skill and little success. Chicoans met on June 26 to demand that the authorities send troops to pacify the area.

Farther north, a group of 10 citizens from the Red Bluff area headed into the hills east of their town. About July 1, they attacked a village in the Antelope Creek drainage during the night, killing a few Indians and claiming to recover clothing from the Hickok children.

Keefer turned to an expert, Hiram "Hi" Good of Tehama County, and paid him to find the killers. Good and three others went into the hills and found the boy's body "by the smell" and brought it back to Chico for burial beside his sisters. He had been tossed from a cliff, Good reported, and stones were thrown down on top of him.

But rumors flew through the valley that the child had been

tortured to death. His fingers and tongue were cut off, some reports said. Others said he was set afire. Still a third version of the tale claimed he'd been staked out and stoned to death by the Indian children.

Good announced plans to chastise the Indians, and set up camp on Deer Creek Flats, a bluff on the south side of that stream about 10 miles upstream from the Sacramento River. He called for volunteers to join him and sought a commission from the state to attack the Indians.

The commission was not forthcoming. In addition, the Chicoans' plea for assistance resulted in nothing more than the delivery of a few rusty and worthless smoothbore muskets from a federal armory.

At this point Chico's founder and most prominent citizen, John Bidwell, appealed directly to Kibbe, and secured a case of modern military rifles for Good and his men. Bidwell also contributed $100 to supply the force.

On July 24, Good and the 15 men who had gathered around him on Deer Creek Flats headed into the Antelope Creek drainage, scattering one village of 200 Indians (undoubtedly an exaggeration) in an attack, killing one. The Indians were tracked to another site and attacked at dawn. Seventeen were reported killed and six were wounded. A number of children were captured and brought out of the hills when Good and company returned to Deer Creek Flats for replenishment in early August.

Good's company returned to the warpath Aug. 11. Two days later, the Indians struck back, hitting the Kelley ranch on Deer Creek. But while the Indian men were so involved, the women and children were apparently an easy catch for the white raiders, who gathered up 21 prisoners at a site on Mill Creek and brought them out on a few days later.

About this time, two companies of the 2nd California Volunteer Cavalry arrived at the request of Bidwell. Good's efforts ended, the cavalry patrolled the hills for a time with no success and a kind of quiet returned.

There was another Indian raid across the valley before August ended. The *Colusa Sun* reported Aug. 30 that Millsaps' ranch on Stony Creek had been attacked. Indians entered the house of John G. Wilson and pelted him with rocks. He was also wounded

Hi Good sits front and center in this undated photo from the Pioneer Museum in Oroville. Good led several raids into Yahi Country following the killing of the Hickok children in June 1862. Flanking Good from left to right are Jay Salisbury, Sandy Young and "Indian Lad." The people in this photo were misidentified in a number of other publications.[1]

with an arrow fired by an Indian named "Pete."

Andrew J. "Dick" Millsaps was one of the members of the Eagle Peak posse earlier in the year.

A new posse formed and pursued the Indians north to Thomes Creek — which flows within about five miles of Eagle Peak — and killed four. Pete was caught and hung by "friendly Indians," the *Sun* reported.

Trouble at Nome Cult

September brought another crisis in Indian-white relations in Northern California. The settlers around Nome Cult Farm in Round Valley made a blatant play to take over the reservation lands, releasing their cattle into the Indians' grain fields and destroying the crops.

The Concow Maidu elder Tome-ya-nem recognized they would starve unless they poached the neighbors' cattle. Yet, if they did that, they would be killed.

So he bid a cordial goodbye to reservation superintendent James Short and headed east with 350 to 400 Indians toward their former homelands in Butte County. Most were Maidu but there were Pit River and Hat Creek Indians also.

Ironically, a year earlier, Tome-ya-nem had led some of the same men who were now going home in an attack on other Indians, at the bequest of the stockmen who now posed such a threat.

In September 1861, a band of several hundred Wailaki Indians had set up camp in Horse Canyon, about 20 miles north of Round Valley, and had begun stealing livestock from ranches in the area.

The force was too big for the settlers in the area to take on. After much persuasion, Tome-ya-nem agreed to take his followers to assist in an attack, in which dozens of Wailaki were killed.

But that was all forgotten by the reservation's neighbors in October 1862, and the Indians needed to flee.

A company of the 2nd California Cavalry chased them down, and gathered them together on the old Nome Lackee Reservation, which was all but abandoned then.

The Indians clearly could not be taken back to Nome Cult until the situation there was resolved. Letting them return freely to Butte County was asking for trouble. So in October the Indian Superintendent for Northern California, George Hanson, turned to probably the only man who could help: John Bidwell.

Bidwell was a prominent pioneer, a member of the first wagon train to cross the continent to California in 1841. A schoolteacher by trade back east, he worked for John Sutter at his fort in present-day Sacramento. He also served in a staff position during the war against Mexico, for which he was awarded the rank of major.

In 1848, he was back working for Sutter when gold was found at Sutter's mill under construction on the American River. Thinking there might also be gold on the Feather River farther north, Bidwell and a couple of partners — with a contingent of Indian laborers — undertook some prospecting there.

The effort, at a place called Bidwell Bar, was phenomenally successful. Bidwell was able to buy about 11,000 acres of the Mexican land grant Rancho Arroyo Chico in 1849, and settled contently on the north bank of Big Chico Creek before the first 49ers struggled over the mountains to the Mother Lode.

Bidwell bought more land throughout the 1850s until his holdings were greater than 30,000 acres. By then he had brought the local Indian tribe, the Mechoopda, onto his ranch to provide labor, and built the Rancho Chico into an agrarian showcase.

He founded the town of Chico in 1860, and by 1862 it had several hundred residents.

Bidwell had the resources to take on the refugees from Nome Cult, but he was wary of doing so. Not all the residents of Chico were fond of him. The June 26 meeting that followed the killing of the Hickok children, for instance, had turned into a verbal fusillade aimed at the town father.

The outbursts were fueled partly by envy of Bidwell's success, and partly by the presence of the Mechoopda on his ranch. A good percentage of the population believed all Indians were in cahoots, and that Bidwell's Indians somehow contributed to the Hickok killings.

The tension was raised further because this was the midst of the Civil War, and Forty-Niners had come from both sides of the Mason-Dixon Line. With the war, neighbors had become adversaries. News of each great battle in the east brought both elation and despair in California.

Bidwell was a stanch unionist, which inflamed the Southerners. And some of the Northerners considered the Rancho Chico uncomfortably similar to a Southern slave plantation, with the Mechoopda substituted for the Africans.

Bidwell had dampened the outright hostility of that summer by showing he was well enough connected to state military officials to get some proper weapons delivered to Hi Good, and well enough connected to federal military officials to get a couple of companies of cavalry sent to the area. He may well have derailed Good's effort to get a state commission to go after the Indians.

Bidwell had made it clear he was not one to be trifled with.

But he understood the tensions still simmered, and that bringing several hundred more Indians onto his ranch couldn't help. There just wasn't any other option.

So Bidwell reluctantly took on Tome-ya-nem's band, on the promise that the federal authorities would take them back to Nome Cult as soon as practical in the spring. The Indians were encamped at the farthest western reach of Rancho Chico, at the old landing on the Sacramento River, which was as far from Chico as Bidwell could place them. A federal special agent, James Eddy, was appointed to oversee the camp.

The year ended, the new year would come, and as soon as practical would turn out to not be soon enough.

NOTE

1. The misidentification of the people in the photo above seems to date to the 1979 publication of *Ishi the Last Yahi*, by Robert Heizer and Theodora Kroeber. I became aware of the error when obtaining a copy of the photo from the Pioneer Museum in 2004 for a newspaper article I was writing for the *Chico Enterprise-Record* and *Red Bluff Daily News*. In some publications since, "Indian Lad" has been rendered as "Indian Ned." Hi Good was killed by an Indian named Ned, who was subsequently killed by Sandy Young.

Chapter 12

The bridge to the site of Helltown in Butte Creek Canyon. The lynching in 1863 of five Indians in the then-mining camp triggered a cycle of revenge and retribution.

1863

The residents of Butte County had reason to be wary of the 350–400 refugees from the Nome Cult Farm who were camped on the Rancho Chico in 1863.

Early in the year, the camp operated by Indian agent James Eddy had been a boon to the area, renting laborers to nearby farms as a way to pay for the costs of housing the Indians. That and a line of credit at John Bidwell's store was all that kept the camp functioning. Washington, D.C., wasn't concerned about the expense of caring for a few hundred Indians 3,000 miles away, with the Civil War raging on the capital's doorstep.

But there were as many Indians in Eddy's camp as there were non-Indians in the relatively new town of Chico. And the Indians had reason to be upset. They'd been forcibly removed from their homelands of thousands of years and shuffled from one site to another. When their new neighbors in Round Valley ran them off, none of the authorities who'd put the Indians there were able to defend them, or perhaps, didn't care to defend them.

At best the Indians were disappointed in the newcomers. However, pent-up anger and rage had to be common and deep among the hundreds gathered on Rancho Chico. There were agitators among them, including the apparently immortal and omnipresent Hat Creek Lize.

The camp was a sleeping bear that reasonable men would not poke.

But despite that, in early June some miners in Butte Creek Canyon decided to lynch five Indians.

The trouble begins

There are several versions of the story, but they are similar at the core.

In early June, a mule went missing in the mining community of Helltown, one of the four mining towns in Butte Creek Canyon. The resident Indians were blamed, and four who were disliked by the miners were picked to die.

An Indian elder, dubbed "Chief Codfish" by the whites in the canyon, protested that there was no evidence connecting the four to the missing mule, and he too was hung with the other four.

And then, as this version of the story is told, the missing mule wandered back into camp.

There was outrage in the newspapers, and threats were made against the lynch mob, but no one seems to have considered taking the matter to court.

It didn't take long for the demands of day-to-day life to become more important than the deaths of five Indians, and in the end, nothing was done. White civilization shrugged it off as just another atrocity against a lesser race, and life went on for those who hadn't been hanged.

For the Indians, that just fueled the outrage.

The miners in the canyon may have felt Butte County's resident Indians could not have mounted a significant response. That is likely true, as their roles were pretty well fixed in the matrix of white civilization.

Many of them had been incorporated into California's new economy. They labored in the mines, or on the farms that were replacing prospecting as gold became scarcer and scarcer. The Indians maintained households and gardens in the towns. Many white men had taken Indian wives in practice if not under the law. That likely included John Bidwell. Several modern-day Mechoopda report a lineage to him.

The native groups that still survived in the foothills, trying to live in the traditional ways, understood the danger of angering the newcomers and tried to keep to themselves. Generally they were tolerated by the newcomers as long as the land they occupied wasn't of much value, and they didn't get too upset by the occasional rape, slave kidnapping or murder.

Although modern writers have labeled the Yahi as the Indian antagonists in what followed the hangings in the canyon, as the "Mill Creeks" figure in accounts of what happened that year. But the Yahi were too distant and isolated to even know what had happened, and too few to have acted anyway.

But about 20 miles away from Helltown in 1863, camped on Bidwell's rancho, there were hundreds of Indians with time on their hands and in many cases, anger in their hearts.

Among them undoubtedly were Nimshews, the Butte Creek Indians who'd been gathered up by Kibbe in 1859. Their kin, including a revered elder, had just been hanged. They were capable of mounting an entirely predictable raid of retribution.

It started July 19 near Forks of Butte when a man named John Hayes was seriously wounded by a band of Indians who had surrounded his cabin. According to a report in an Oroville newspaper, two or three of his "domestic squaws" were slain at the same time.

The newspaper continued that John Stammer was shot in the arm later that day near Jaggard's Mill, a little above Dogtown, just up the hill from Forks of Butte.

The next day miner Richard Morrison was killed on the West

Branch of the Feather River, a mile above Dogtown. Later that day and farther down the river a Mrs. Blum was shot through the thigh near Kunkle Reservoir. She was pregnant and was later reported to have born a healthy child a few months later before dying of her wound.

"Of the cause of the present outbreak, and the massacre of peaceful inhabitants ... we are unadvised," the *Butte Record* commented on July 25, "but fear that the hanging of five Indians recently, at Helltown, on suspicion of having committed depredations upon property, has incited them to retaliate by murdering those who fall into their hands ..."

It was the final act of the Indian raid that would have the most impact.

The Lewis children

On July 21, three children of Sam and Mary Ann Lewis were returning from school to their home in Berry Canyon, the gulch of Little Dry Creek. It's just west of today's Butte College campus, up Williams Road.

The three were Jimmy, 11, Thankful, 9, and Johnny, 6.

Johnny wanted a drink of water, and they headed to Little Dry Creek, picking a spot unfortunately close to where members of the Indian raiding party were hiding in some grape vines.

A shot rang out, and Jimmy pitched forward into the creek, shot in the back, according to Thankful's account, *Captured by the Mill Creek Indians,* which was published in 1915.

The Indians pelted his body with stones to make sure he was dead, Thankful wrote, and one, "The Big Foot Indian," took Jimmy's hat as his own.

Big Foot is one of the legendary Indians of this era, on a par with Hat Creek Lize. He seemed to have been involved in most of the atrocities in the neighborhood. Thankful described him as having one big foot and one small foot; other accounts give him six toes on one or both of his feet.

Thankful also described two of the Indians as "terrible to look at," with their heads tarred. That was a practice of some California Indians related to mourning, which supports the idea this was a raid of revenge for the Helltown lynchings.

Marker in the Clear Creek Cemetery, south of Paradise east of Clark Road, identifies this as the site where Jimmy and John Lewis were buried after being killed by the "Mill Creek Indians" in 1863. However, the Lewis family plot is some distance away.

All told there were 10 Indians, and they took Thankful and her young brother north, spending the night in Nance Canyon, north of Neal Road.

In the morning before dawn the raiders pushed on with Thankful. Little Johnny, who had "commenced to fret" according to Thankful, was held back and killed.

The trek continued north, with one Indian leaving the group at one point to head down into the valley. "He was not a Mill Creek Indian," Thankful wrote, "but was supposed to have been one from the rancheria." This is undoubtedly a reference to Eddy's encampment on Bidwell's rancho.

The group ended up in Big Chico Creek Canyon, and in a confusing turn of events, Thankful appeared to have been left in the company of a single Indian, who in my reading of her account, seems to have allowed her to escape.

Aftermath

The death of the Lewis boys sent groups of armed whites rampaging through the countryside seeking Indian blood. That included Sam Lewis, who led a party into Chico, picked out two Indians they didn't like, and executed them for the death of his sons.

Bands of frightened Indians flocked to their few white friends, seeking protection.

On July 27 a meeting was held at Pence's Ranch, quite close to where the Lewis children had been killed, and a resolution was passed, giving Butte County's Indians 30 days to surrender to be sent to a reservation, or they would be killed.

Federal Indian Superintendent George Hanson and Bidwell

attended the meeting and unsuccessfully attempted to calm the crowd of 300 men, whom Hanson described as "infuriated."

Bidwell was one of the objects of their fury. He was resented by some for his success. Others brought to California by the Gold Rush from what had become Confederacy resented his unwavering support of the unionists.

The mob demanded that the Mechoopda, Bidwell's labor force, be included in the Indian exclusion, which he staunchly opposed.

Upon his return to Chico, Bidwell told the Mechoopda to "run to the river" and hide in the forest there, clearly feeling they were at risk.

But Bidwell was a man of influence, and on Aug. 1, 40 soldiers of Company F of the 2nd California Cavalry arrived in Chico, ostensibly to transport the Indians to the reservation. There's little doubt their actual role was to protect Bidwell, his Indian labor force, and his ranch. Within a month, two more companies would arrive at Rancho Chico.

Meanwhile vigilante groups were combing the hills and valley to take any Indians found to Eddy's camp. Far more were coming in voluntarily, fearing the rising hostility in Butte County. Nine murders were documented.

Leaders of the vigilante sweep claimed they had gathered in excess of 400 Indians, but that number is likely inflated. A total about half that seems more reasonable. Another 200 to 300 who surrendered to sympathetic settlers were added to that total. Add in the 350 to 400 original inhabitants of Eddy's camp and there should have been 800 to 900 Indians there.

Yet when the Indians left Chico Sept. 4 en route to Nome Cult, there were only 461 Indians in the camp. Undoubtedly some had escaped, but the majority had been killed by an outbreak of "bilious fever" — apparently malaria — which had swept through the camp. People were dying every day, and most of the others were ill to one degree or another.

They were not in any condition to be moved, but the tension in Butte County was such that they could not stay.

The Nome Cult Trail

What followed is Northern California's own Trail of Tears.

Dozens died from malaria along the trail across the valley, and when the exodus reached the foot of the Coast Range mountains, about 150 were too sick to proceed. A temporary infirmary was set up for them at a place called Mountain House.

The rest tried to press on over the mountains, but many of them were unable to and were left to their fate beside the trail. Only 80 made it to Nome Cult.

Troops went back to bring in all who survived along the trail or at Mountain House. There's no final count on how many finally made it to the reservation, but it's safe to say at least half of the Indians died between Chico and Nome Cult.

Most of the Mechoopda appear to have been missing from the convoy, as a result of Bidwell's efforts to get soldiers sent to the ranch. About 100 of the soldiers who had been deployed in August remained in town to deal with expected attacks by vigilantes upon the Rancho Chico because of the Indians who remained.

The attacks did not happen, largely due to the garrison, but also in recognition Bidwell was likely to keep close watch on his workers, who were undoubtedly terrified of their neighbors. They weren't likely to cause trouble and weren't worth the risk an attack would have posed.

Bidwell would be named a brigadier general of the California militia later in September.

Chapter 13

The killings of two white women in Shasta County in 1864 were attributed to the Antelope Creek Indians. Antelope Creek Canyon, shown here, is not as extreme as Mill Creek or Deer Creek canyons, but after the Yahi had retreated from it, it still provided sanctuary for renagades.

1864

Ever since outsiders began flooding into California with the Gold Rush, there had been regular calls for wars of "extermination" against the native population. Some of the residents of Shasta County gave that a try in 1864, when the Mill Creek War moved north.

As many as 500 Indians — Yana and Wintun — were killed in response to the killing of two white women in early September east of Redding.

Two large groups of men spent about a month killing any Indians they could find, whether they posed a risk or not, and without concern whether they were connected in any way to the white women's deaths.

There had been raids attributed to Indians leaving the reservation earlier in the year in Butte County. The *Oroville Union Record* and Wells and Chambers' *History of Butte County* reported the looting of a cabin near Dogtown on March 1, and the wounding of a teamster in the vicinity. In early June another home near the Pence Ranch in Butte Valley was raided. A few days later a man was found dead, pierced with four arrows in Potter's Ravine, a few miles farther south.

But there is no report of retaliation, and the news accounts of those incidents was eclipsed by what happened farther north.

The killing started with Catherine Allen, on Sept. 8 at the family home on Old Cow Creek, about 10 miles east of Millville. She was having lunch with her four children, Lilly, 5, John, 3, James, 2, and Robert, 7 months.

The husband and father, William Allen, was stacking hay a few miles to the west.

Two Indians entered the house, were ordered out by Mrs. Allen and a struggle ensued. Mrs. Allen grappled with the larger of the Indians, clutching at the beads around his neck while he pulled her hair. The smaller Indian ended the fuss by shooting Mrs. Allen in the head. She fell to the floor dead, a handful of Indian beads locked in her death grip.

The Indians then attacked the children, beating the elder three with a gun. Robert was picked up by the feet, and his head was bashed against the hearth.

At the time, the wounds inflicted on the children were believed to be fatal. The newspapers went so far as to report two of them dead. Yet, all of them survived.

A hole was broken in Robert's skull by the blow to the hearth, and the doctor who attended to him was supposed to have placed a silver 50-cent piece to cover the gap. In later years, after the wound had healed over the coin, Robert was reported to have said he could never be completely broke, that he always had 50 cents.

The next day the wife of Arkansas Jones was killed at her home near Copper City, which now lies beneath the Pit River arm of Shasta Lake.

Again, the husband was away, hunting squirrels in this case. An Indian approached a neighbor's 8-year-old daughter who was visiting and grabbed her, threatening to kill her. Mrs. Jones, hearing the girl's screams, ran out to intervene and was shot in the head. The little girl escaped and looked back to count 12 or 13 Indians.

Mr. Jones returned to find his fatally injured wife, who had been shot in the face with a number of arrows and partially scalped, according to history compiled by May Southern, founder of the Shasta Historical Society.

The attacks have been attributed to the Yahi ever since Thomas Waterman concluded they were "certainly" responsible in his *The Yana Indians.*

The Yahi were almost certainly not responsible, however.

Newspaper accounts at the time blamed the attacks on the Antelope Indians. The Antelope Creek drainage had at one time been Yahi country. But the area, while rough, was less extreme than Deer and Mill Creek canyons, and was dangerously accessible to the newcomers. Lumber mills had been operating there since the 1850s.

By 1864 the area wasn't safe for the Yahi and wasn't needed for the tribe's greatly reduced numbers. It was another of those voids that hadn't yet been filled with the newcomers, and so provided a degree of sanctuary for renegade bands.

The blame was set precisely by Jeremiah Curtin, who was the first to write a comprehensive history of the events, in his 1898 *Creation Myths of Primitive America.*

"Certain Indians lived, or rather lurked around Mill Creek, in wild places somewhat east of Tehama and north of Chico. These Mill Creek Indians were fugitives; outlaws from various tribes, among others from the Yana."

But the white war parties that formed after the killings didn't really care who was responsible. They just wanted to kill any Indian they could find.

The *Shasta Courier* newspaper reported 40 men from Copper City had gathered and about that same number from Millville and Cow Creek. The newspaper reported they were "bent on extermination and are indiscriminately killing all of Indian blood."

In some cases, Indians were tracked down to hideaways in the foothills and mountains, but the vigilantes also appear to have gone from homestead to homestead and killed any Indian domestic or farm help they could find.

There was no one in the area like John Bidwell, with a large Indian labor force and the influence to get soldiers sent to protect it. The Indians in eastern Shasta County were in small groups, one, two or a handful attached to a white household. They were totally at the mercy of the dozens of armed men who went from ranch to ranch, having left mercy behind.

Curtin tells the story of a Yana girl named Eliza, "industrious and much liked by those who knew her," who was working for a farmer north of Millville when the gunmen came for her.

A leader of the band had worked for Eliza's employer and she was said to have begged him, "Don't kill me; when you were here I cooked for you, I washed for you, I was kind to you; I never asked pay of you; don't kill me now."

She was shot 11 times, according to Curtin. Then afterward the killers all took a drink, and their leader smashed Eliza's skull with his rifle butt.

Curtin also reports 300 Indians were killed at a religious gathering up in Oak Run, a number that sounds unlikely, especially since the incident was not reported in the newspapers at the time.

The newspapers did report a massacre in a cave in the Antelope Creek country in late September, a story that has taken interesting twists in the retelling.

Newspaper accounts indicate the Copper City and Millville crews had merged and killed 13 Indians in a cave, recovering seven rifles and finding women's and children's clothing.

May Southern's account says the Indians were located at a cave on Mill Creek, but the raiders dropped back to make an attack at daylight. By then, their target was gone, though they'd left behind sugar, beef and flour. That was laced with strychnine.

"A large number of skulls found in the Mill Creek cave a few years later bears testimony that they died. Mrs. Jones' gold buckle was found in the cave."

The slaughter had all happened east of the Sacramento River, but in early October Arkansas Jones also led a group of 30 raiders west of the river, not intending to kill Indians unless they were across the river at the time of the Allen and Jones killings. Eight Indians were killed in a campaign that went as far as the Trinity River.

On Oct. 8, the residents of Millville gathered to approve a written resolution giving all Indians 10 days to get out of the area east of the Sacramento River, from below Antelope Creek to the Pit River.

"Resolved: That if any Indians are found within the boundaries of the first resolution it shall be the privilege of our company or citizens to exterminate or expel said Indians."

Three days later a rival meeting was held at Churntown, in present-day Redding, by citizens who called the Millville resolution "inconsistent with humanity" and vowed to fight its implementation.

But it was largely irrelevant. Almost all of the Indians who were subjects of the resolutions had already been killed.

Chapter 14

My opinion is that the Three Knolls are the three bald knobs across the low center of this photo, which is looking south. Mill Creek lies behind them. Beyond that is the ridge that separates Mill Creek from Boat Gunwale Creek. The Lassen Trail ran down the ridge on the distant horizon. This picture was taken from the saddle between Black Oak Grove and Table Mountain in Mill Creek Canyon.

1865: The misplaced massacres

Central to the story of the Yahi's destruction are two oft-cited massacres, in both of which more than 30 Indians were said to have been killed. They were the Three Knolls and Kingsley Cave.

There are some glaring problems in the accounts of both slaughters, which in my reasoned opinion have resulted in them being mapped in places where they didn't happen.

The following two chapters will attempt to explain my conclusion that two massacres happened in the summer of 1865 in

Mill Creek Canyon, a few miles and a few weeks apart.

Both attacks used similar tactics, and their proximity in time and space allowed them to be entangled and confused.

In mid-August 1865, a group of renegades from the Nome Cult Reservation were attacked at a site beneath three knolls on the north side of Mill Creek, a few miles downstream from Black Rock.

A few weeks later, the remainder of the Yahi were dealt a fatal blow at their last real village, on Mill Creek a few miles upstream from Black Rock.

That was the slaughter incorrectly placed at Kingsley Cave. And it was incorrectly named for the massacre that happened few weeks earlier under the three knolls a dozen miles downstream.

We'll begin with the Three Knolls.

Concow and the Three Knolls

There had been little conflict with the Indians in Butte County in 1864, as might have been expected in light of the expulsion of the native people that followed the killing of the Lewis children the previous year.

But in 1865, the Mill Creek War returned to south of Yahi country, with a bloody raid by Indians, followed by an attack of retribution that has become known as the Three Knolls Massacre.

It's the best-documented massacre of the war, with four detailed accounts published — one just days after the attack — and a brief newspaper item.

And yet, there is much about the incident that was left unsettled, including where it happened, how many people were killed, and the identity of those who were slain.

This is how the story has been told up to now: In revenge for a raid by "Mill Creeks" in the Concow Valley, southeast of present-day Paradise, a group of whites tracked the raiders to a village on Mill Creek upstream from Black Rock where the entire Yahi nation was gathered. More than 30 of the Indians were killed (the number varies), with only five or six escaping.

The implication has been that the survivors were Ishi's companions at the time their final hiding place was found in 1908. Theodora Kroeber wrote that Ishi's father was among those killed in the attack, even though she also said Ishi refused to talk about the incident, so it's unclear how she determined that.

But it's a story that breaks down almost immediately when you look back to the primary sources, and think about what they actually wrote.

To begin with, the Concow Valley is dozens of miles from Yahi country, much farther than the severely pressed Yahi could have mounted an offensive.

The sources include a Concow man named Daniel Klauberg, who wrote a detailed account of the expedition a few days afterward that was published in the *Butte Record*. That account is included in this volume.

Robert Anderson described the raid in *Fighting the Mill Creeks*.

Sim Moak wrote a long letter to his father and mother that November recounting the raid, and also included an account in his *Last of the Mill Creeks*.

Hi Good went and talked to the Red Bluff newspaper shortly after the attack.

Patching together the story from the various accounts, we can determine the trouble began on Monday, Aug. 7, 1865. At about 6 p.m., a party of three to five Indians appeared at the Robert Workman house in the Concow Valley. Mrs. Workman and her sister, Miss Mary Rosanna Smith, fled into the house, but the Indians followed, forcing their way in.

Mrs. Workman ran out the back, apparently to call for the aid of the hired hand, John Banks. A pursuing Indian caught up to her as she left the house and knocked her down with a blow from a rifle butt. The Indian aimed the rifle at her, but turned the muzzle toward Banks as he came running up and shot him dead. The Indian then picked up a large rock, crashed it down on Mrs. Workman's chest, and left her for dead.

The raiders then apparently turned their attentions to Miss Smith, who was "ravished." Her throat was cut and her body was mutilated. Banks also had his throat cut, but Mrs. Workman escaped that fate, escaping to a place of safety while the Indians were otherwise distracted.

The house was ransacked, and the raiders making off with gold coin valued at about $2,500, a silk dress, thread and other items.

Mrs. Workman made her way about 200 yards to the home of G.G. Marquis, and was taken to the Porter Quartz Mill, where the residents of the valley were gathering in fear.

The *Butte Union Record* reports there were only four men in the valley at the time of the raid, the rest being at a political convention in Oroville.

The Indians don't appear to have felt much threatened, as they lingered in the area until Wednesday morning, Aug. 9, when they shot and wounded Joseph Miller near Frenchtown, a now-gone town that then lay in the eastern end of the valley. Two other houses were reportedly robbed, and one was burned down.

But by Wednesday afternoon, Aug. 9, the white settlers had a posse of six or eight men together and started in pursuit. The trail led to the northwest, toward Chico. By Thursday night, the group was camped at Butte Mills, very near the current Butte Creek Country Club.

As they continued north the following day, they ran into Sim Moak, who decided to join the raiders after hearing their tale. Moak rode ahead toward Solomon Gore's house on Rock Creek, near the foot of the Cohasset Ridge, intending to raise a party and block the Indian crossing of that stream.

He was too late. The raiders had come and gone.

The Concow men arrived at Gore's about noon on Friday, Aug. 11, and were joined by a number of young men from the area, including Gore's son-in-law, Robert Anderson. The reinforced group moved on to Hi Good's place on Deer Creek and camped for the night.

Good killed a sheep for the raiders to eat, and John Bidwell sent up 40 pounds of bacon and 40 pounds of hardtack for the campaign ahead.

On Saturday morning, Aug. 12, the party headed into the hills, crossing Deer Creek Flats — a bluff overlooking that stream — and descending into Deer Creek Canyon. They moved upstream a few miles and camped for the night near the foot of Iron Mountain.

Anderson said the next day the group moved north and crossed the "two dry creeks."

This clearly locates the massacre site as downstream from

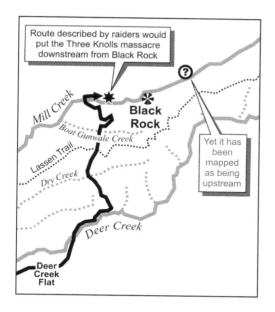

Route described by raiders would put the Three Knolls massacre downstream from Black Rock

Yet it has been mapped as being upstream

Black Rock. That's because no creeks have to be crossed moving from Deer Creek to Mill Creek in the vicinity of the monolith and upstream. The two streams press closer together in that stretch and the secondary drainages all run north-south into the larger streams.

However downstream from Black Rock, Mill and Deer creeks veer apart, and a number of smaller seasonal streams flow to the west. The two Anderson seems to be talking about appear to be Dry Creek and Boat Gunwale Creek, both of which are dry in August.

The current trail from Deer Creek to Mill Creek follows that route, dipping into the two canyons that are in the neighborhood of 1,000 feet deep. Between, they cross the Lassen Trail, through a gap in the ridge the emigrant road runs down.

If the raiders were headed upstream from Black Rock they most certainly would have turned east at that point and followed the road.

Some have seized on a comment Moak attributed to Anderson, that he was sure the Indians were at Black Rock, to label one or another of the sites around that basalt block as the Three Knolls. But that doesn't make sense. If the village was there, why would Anderson refer to a trio of landmarks that are so obscure that he and Good disagreed on which side of the creek they were on, instead of identifying the village by the obvious and dominating reference point Black Rock provides?

At the Lassen Trail, one man — Joseph Dikeman — gave out and turned toward back the valley. The 16 who remained pressed on, crossing Boat Gunwale Canyon and coming to the ridge overlooking Mill Creek. They were about a mile from the creek at this time, several miles downstream from Black Rock.

As they moved down an open ridge toward the creek, Anderson noted an Indian picket across the stream, at a lush area low on a bluff. The description matches an area on Long Point where a series of springs would provide a nice little oasis even today, if range cattle hadn't torn up the area badly, leaving it a muck hole.

The raiders turned back, wound behind a high point in the ridge and followed the cover of a gully down to Mill Creek. The route gets a little vague here, as there are at least three watercourses that fit the general description. The paths all lead to the south side of the creek between Long Point and Table Mountain, the area I believe the Yahi called Tuliyani. (See Chapter 4.)

There's a point about the terrain here worth noting. There's not much flat ground on the north side of the creek in this area. Instead the bluffs rise up steeply for a few hundred feet, and then flatten out, climbing more gradually to the next divide. That higher table is divided by several smaller creeks into three ridges. Viewed from many points on the surrounding higher ground, the ends of these ridges look like three knolls rising out of the trees in the creek bottom.

I'm not certain this is what Anderson meant. The reference is so strange, as Mill Creek Canyon is so extreme and so dramatic that the idea a knoll could be a landmark is tough to believe. These three ridges are at least significant enough to serve as landmarks, and they really do provide one of the better ways to identify the area I believe is Tuliyani.

The reference is clearer than any other trio of humps or bumps in Yahi country.

The ridges/knolls also match the description of Klauberg. He doesn't mention knolls, but says they camped on a ridge opposite the camp and moved down both sides of an adjacent ridge to launch the attack.

And down along Mill Creek in this area is a location that matches the descriptions of the massacre site exactly. There's a lens-shaped gravel and sandbar beneath a high bank, with a natural ford at the downstream end of the flat. It is just as Anderson, Moak and Klauberg described the site.

At any rate, the raiders came to the creek downstream from

California Department of Forestry archaeologist Richard Jenkins moves a metal detector over the presumed site of the Three Knolls massacre after a hike to the location in the 1990s. Nothing dating to the 1860s was found.

the site, crossed over and rested in some reeds while Anderson and Good scouted around. They saw some Indian women headed upstream and returned to their group. It was about dark when the raiders followed the women upstream, moving uphill away from the creek to avoid detection.

They stopped on a slope, and Anderson and Good again went scouting to find the Indian camp. They waded up the creek to the point where an Indian's dog challenged them. Anderson describes Indians sitting up from bedrolls around campfires on the sandbar, then settling back down to sleep.

Here's the second major problem of the traditional version of this story. The Three Knolls Massacre has been represented in the histories thus far as an attack on an established village. It is a mistake I made for quite a few years.

But the slaughter, the participants' accounts agree, happened on a gravel and sandbar, a feature born of submersion under high water. The Yahi weren't dumb enough to build a village in a flood plain. They didn't have the time or resources to build structures that would just be washed away with the next predictable flood.

This was not an attack on an established village, but rather on the temporary camp of a group of Indians on the move.

But still, Anderson quotes Sandy Young as saying he'd passed through the massacre scene later in 1865 and reported it looked like a cyclone had hit. It's hard to imagine that description applying to an attack on an overnight camp where there would have been little more than bedrolls and campfires.

Young was John Bidwell's representative in Big Meadows, now submerged under Lake Almanor. He led an expedition down Mill Creek in 1865 in response to raids by the Mill Creeks on the Mountain Maidu who were partially his responsibility, as many of them were employed building Bidwell's Humboldt Road from Chico to Susanville.

At any rate, the Three Knolls raiders moved a few hundred yards back to pass the night.

As the eastern sky began to lighten on the morning of Monday, Aug. 14, 1865, the white raiders began to move toward their sleeping targets. Sim Moak and Frank Curtis were sent off upstream to block the Indians' escape in that direction. William Merithew (his name also appears as Merathew and Matthews) moved to the creek downstream from the village.

The remainder spread into a loose half-circle and moved down the ridge toward the sleeping Indians. Good and Hardy Thomasson were in the center of the line on the west side of the ridge. Anderson and Henry Curtis held the middle of those on the eastern slope. Klauberg, judging from his observations, was with Good.

They were a few dozen yards from the village when an early-rising Indian came climbing up the slope toward them. He was recognized as Billy Sims, a valley Indian gone bad, Anderson reported. It's easy to imagine him stopping, stunned, as he saw the whites creeping down the hill at him in the pale light before dawn.

He recognized Anderson and aimed his rifle at him. Henry Curtis whistled a warning and Anderson ducked behind a tree. Sims bolted, not to warn the village, but to escape across the ford to the other side of the creek. He was fighting across the current when Good shot him through the breast. Sims struggled on to the other bank, staggered along the shore for a few steps, and collapsed.

The white raiders then ran to the bank above the sandbar and fired as fast as they could at the Indians who were scrambling for safety just below them. Many ran for the ford. Others headed for the cottonwoods and alders along the creek bank and headed upstream.

The slaughter was limited by one or more Indian riflemen who appeared on a bluff on the opposite side of the creek and began firing at the white attackers. The settlers scrambled for cover, and most of the Indians escaped in the interim. Anderson said he put a shot into the rocks between one of the Indian sniper's legs, and when he staggered back under cover, the camp belonged to the whites.

That the Indians had firearms reinforce the idea that the targets of the raid were not Yahi. In addition to bullets, the white raiders were serenaded with eloquent curses in English. When Ishi came out of the wild, he knew no English words, and one could presume that would be the case for the entire tribe.

Good and Thomasson splashed across the ford to secure the opposite bank, cutting off an Indian woman's escape in the process. She was taken prisoner.

Good scalped Sims and recrossed the creek to take the scalps from the four or five Indians laying dead there. That was his right as the captain of the company. The men from Concow, wrought up by the rape and mutilation of Miss Smith, were mutilating the bodies. One Indian's neck was cut to the bone, with the head being twisted around afterward in an unnatural way.

But here's another problem: The number of dead reported by the participants didn't approach the 30 cited in the common version of the Three Knolls attack.

Good put the number at nine in an account published in the Red Bluff Independent three days after the account. Klauberg said there were five bodies on the field and six or seven who escaped but "will surely die." Moak agrees with the body count of five, and further identifies them as a man, two women and two children.

The toll in excess of 30 appears to stem from a comment W.J. Seagraves made to Thomas Waterman when he was collecting information for his 1918 paper *The Yana Indians*.

Seagraves said he'd visited the scene years after and there were about 40 to 45 skeletons still scattered on the surface.

Waterman singled out Seagraves as one of his best informants, which leaves us another mystery to resolve. How could a trusted informant count far more dead than those who had participated in the attack?

Back at the Three Knolls, the attackers rifled through the Indians' effects. They found a native infant alive, who Good promptly claimed. The boy, Anderson reported, had six toes on his feet.

One wonders if he may have been the son of a notorious Indian raider, a man the whites called Big Foot. He had large feet, with six toes on each. His distinctive tracks were often found at the scene of Indian "depredations," but after the Three Knolls Massacre, they were seen no more. He may have been shot while crossing the stream and floated away. Or he may have succumbed to wounds which allowed him to flee the carnage before dying.

The raiders gathered up such plunder as they could carry and burned the rest. The captive woman was forced to carry the infant, and the group headed off toward the Sacramento Valley.

Anderson reported they "climbed the long hill and over its crest into Twenty-Mile Hollow." This is another indication the three knolls weren't upstream from Black Rock, as Twenty-Mile Hollow is about a dozen miles downhill from there. There's no way you could go over the crest of a long hill into the hollow from Black Rock or upstream from there. You'd cross the crest several miles' walk away from the hollow.

At the top of the hollow, the woman refused to go farther and was killed. The raiders continued down into the valley, with the Concow men moving on toward Chico. John Bidwell sent a wagon to carry them to town and bought them dinner at the fanciest spot in town — Weatherbee's hotel. He then provided them a ride back to Concow, where they arrived in glory, we can presume.

Anderson and Moak say the Indians were "chastised" to the point they presented only minor troubles to the settlers from then on. This ignores the murder of Mrs. Dersch the following year, but that was up in Shasta County, a long way from Chico in those days.

But it may not have just been the Three Knolls attack that brought peace to the vicinity. The discrepancies about the location, the death toll, whether a village or a temporary overnight camp was struck, and whether the victims were Yahi or someone else, beg an answer.

After years of thinking about it, I've come to the conclusion that accounts of two separate but similar attacks were blended together by Waterman. That error was widely distributed by Kroeber and has become the "common knowledge" today.

Daniel Klauberg's account follows here. The next chapter will move on to the second attack, the one long misplaced at Kingsley Cave.

Chapter 14 appendix

The Three Knolls are actually the ends of three ridges extending toward Mill Creek from the north. From the air, they don't look anything like knolls; that illusion can only be seen from the ground

Klauberg's Account

The chapter on the Three Knolls massacre is drawn from five primary accounts:

Daniel Klauberg of Concow Valley, where the raid that started the sequence occurred, wrote a long letter to the *Butte Union Record* dated Aug. 20, 1865 — just six days after the Three Knolls — that was published on Aug. 26 of that year. It has not been widely circulated so it is reprinted in its entirety below.

Simeon (Sim) Moak wrote two accounts of the attack, the first in a letter to his parents dated Nov. 21, 1865. The letter, one of several Moak letters that was in the possession of the Gold Nugget Museum in Paradise, Butte County, was published in the December 2006 edition of the museum's *Tales of the Ridge*. That is fortunate, as the museum was destroyed in the Camp Fire of November 2018.

Moak's better-known version of the raid appeared in his book *Last of the Mill Creeks and Early Life in California*, published in 1923. Excerpts were included in *Ishi the Last Yahi: A Documentary History*, compiled by Robert F. Heizer and Theodora Kroeber and first printed in 1979.

Robert Anderson's *Fighting the Mill Creeks*, first published in 1909, includes a long account of the attack. It was also reprinted in Ishi the Last Yahi.

In addition, Hi Good reported the attack immediately after returning home, and word got to the *Red Bluff Independent* in time to publish this article in its Aug. 17 edition:

AN INDIAN FIGHT: News reached Tehama on Tuesday that Capt. H.A. Good and company consisting of 17 men in all who were organized to follow and chastise the Indians who committed the murders in Concow Valley, Butte County, got on the trail of the savages and came up on them Saturday night on Mill Creek, about 16 miles east of this place. The company surrounded the Indians camp, numbering about 50 Indians on Saturday night and attacked them yesterday (Monday) morning. The Indians broke through the ranks and fled, leaving 9 dead and carrying off a great number of wounded, but Capt. Good had no means of ascertaining how many.

Here's the Klauberg account:

BUTTE UNION RECORD Oroville; Saturday, 26 Aug. 1865

A Trip in the Mountains and Fight with the Indians
Concow, Aug. 20, 1865

After the massacre, we stopped in due respect to bury the dead; and on Wednesday, August 9th, started in pursuit of the savages who committed the hellish deed.

Arriving at Spanishtown, more men joined us, and on Thursday we reached Butte Mills — about 25 miles distant — where we camped for the night. In the morning, we received a few lines from Chico, stating where the rest of the boys were heading.

Reached Mr. Gore's place at noon, 12 miles, and made the acquaintance of the celebrated Indian hunter, Robert Anderson; solicited his company to hunt the raiders, which he readily agreed to; and as we were not prepared, he furnished a sack of flour.

From thence we went to Hiram Goode's, another celebrated Indian fighter on Deer Creek, who took command of our company. Here, on a Friday afternoon, we found quite a number of our boys, with an allowance of provisions which came from Gen. Bidwell's, free of charge. Capt. Goode killed a sheep, which we ate at one meal; and, dividing 40 pounds of bacon and 40 pounds of crackers between 17 men, started early Saturday morning for the mountains.

We here found the roughest country that a white man ever traveled over, the whole of it being composed of what geologists term "water made cement." All the various watercourses have formed channels through the different strata of sand and gravel, the bluffs on either side being perpendicular and impassible, except for a few "passes" that were known to Capt. Goode.

We traveled up the south side of Deer Creek 15 miles — then crossing the canyon, traveled 10 miles further up the creek, where we camped. Here we found where the "mahalas" had camped while the "bucks" were out on the raid. We found a cave in the bluff, where were a splendid saddle and bridle and the remains of a horse, which the Indian bandits had no doubt taken from some one on one of their marauding expeditions.

A part of a shawl was picked up here, which was recognized as belonging to one of the girls who was murdered on Rock Creek, four years ago.

Sunday morning, we left Deer Creek canyon and made our way toward Mill Creek. Here the Indians appeared to travel very carelessly and slow, occasionally stopping to eat pine nuts, plums, etc.; they no doubt believed they were now safe from pursuit.

About noon, we struck the "old Lassen trail," crossing it; at this point one of our boys gave out and turned back.

As we approached Mill Creek canyon, Anderson discovered an Indian scout on the other side, watching the trail, but who did not discover us. We hastily marched to one side, and Capt.

Goode and Anderson went on "the scout," crawling through the brush to a point where they could observe the movements of the Indian scout.

In two hours, they returned; we resumed our march, crossing Mill Creek canyon and stopped to eat dinner in the tall grass and brush on the bank, while Goode and Anderson went on another scout and discovered two squaws gathering pine nuts; they watched them and saw where they entered the creek.

About 10 o'clock in the night, we marched to a favorable ridge, right opposite where the Indians had camped. Capt. Goode pulled off his boots and crawled down to the Indian camp, and found precisely where they were, and then came back.

As soon as the sky in the east began to show day was coming, we took up our line of march in two divisions — Anderson taking the left and Goode the right of the ridge — and crawled down within short gun shot of the Indians, and laid 10 minutes longer, when Goode fired his rifle and shot an Indian "buck" through. This was the signal for us to commence.

The Indians were completely surprised and broke for a ford in great confusion. We ran up within 25 yards and all of our guns were brought into action, and just as they came up on the other side, the Indians began to fall thick and fast, some rolling down into the creek and floating off; others crawling into the brush, their trails plainly marked with blood.

While we were fighting the ones who crossed the ford, three Indians had crossed the stream above and with their guns began to make our boys keep out of exposed positions. They were finally dislodged by some one of the boys, as his gun cracked, one of the Indians did a complete summersault and crawled into the brush, which gave us undisputed possession of the battlefield.

Strange to say, none of our boys were hit. There were about 25 Indians; we left five of these killed on the spot, and as many as six or seven who will surely die, and they are nearly all wounded more or less.

When we came to the Indians' camp, we found but few of the articles that had been taken; they had mostly been left, probably, somewhere in the edge of the foothills or in caves on Deer Creek; our provisions being exhausted, we could not hunt them up.

We found a portion of one of Mrs. Workman's dresses, some

skeins of silk and other articles, which were identified by Mrs. Workman. We also found one rifle and one Colt's revolver; the rifle was recognized as belonging to a man in the foothills whose house had been robbed.

Returning homeward, on Tuesday we reached Pine Creek, where a gentleman with a hack took us free of charge to Mud Creek; here Gen. Bidwell's team met us and took us to Chico, and we stopped at Johnson and Weatherbees free of charge, and they rode to Pence's in Bidwell's conveyance, free of charge, and then "footed it" home.

We send our sincere thanks to all those who accommodated us and all who hunted Indians. And the women of Concow send their special thanks to Capt. Hiram Goode, Robert Anderson, and all the Indian hunters.

— *Daniel Klauberg*

Chapter 15

The author's wife Laura at Kingsley Cave. It's long been regarded as the site of a massacre of the Yahi, but there's significant evidence the massacre didn't happen here.

1865: The end of the Yahi

The Kingsley Cave Massacre may be the best known of the slaughters in Yahi country, due to the comments attributed to Norman Kingsley, one of the participants.

He is quoted as being disturbed by how badly his .56-caliber Spencer rifle "tore up" the babies he was shooting with it. Because of that, he used his .38-caliber pistol instead.

The idea that compassion can be measured in caliber is appalling to us today, and the quote sticks in our minds.

That may be the reason the story of the massacre doesn't get critical scrutiny. It's a comment so striking that the story around it just becomes secondary. The story is just supporting material for what today is called a "soundbite."

The lurid quote seems to provide a quick insight to the way people apparently thought back then, without requiring any thought or research. But it is more than a bit suspect. Norman Kingsley died in 1893, long before Thomas Waterman began collecting information. Frank Norvell is the one who recounted it to Waterman.

But it's the way most people today want to regard the pioneers of that era. As a result, we haven't seemed to notice that the story, as it is commonly told, doesn't make any sense.

The massacre supposedly happened in April 1871. Norvell told Waterman that Kingsley and two others were rounding up cattle at a place called Wild Horse Corral, said to be in the Morgan Valley.

They came upon a cow that had been killed and crudely butchered, with chunks of meat hacked out of it, and the hide torn off afterward.

With a dog, they tracked the culprits to a cave holding 30-some Indians, who were cornered and slaughtered. About a ton of dried meat was found in the cave after the killing was done.

The story was recorded by Waterman in his 1918 paper *The Yana Indians*, with the mention that there was a Kingsley Cave just over the ridge from Wild Horse Corral.

However Waterman also reported that pioneer settler Solomon Gore said he'd visited Kingsley Cave shortly after April 1871, and there was no sign of a massacre there.

In the 1950s the University of California at Berkeley decided to check out the story by excavating Kingsley Cave. The dig discovered 30-some burials there, but it was clear they were not of the same date. Graves were found dug through earlier, presumably forgotten burials.

More importantly, the UC dig provided conclusive evidence there was no massacre at the site: They found no bullets. The fusillade required to kill more than 30 Indians would have left a lot of lead in the soil, and the bullets would have turned up in the excavation screens.

The .56-caliber Spencer bullets — bigger than a half-inch in bore — would have been hard to miss.

The Berkeley excavation wasn't the kind of dig conducted

today. Modern archaeologists recognize that every hole dug into a site destroys the historical record of that unit. Therefore, they scatter the excavations across the site to get a sample of what lies beneath the soil.

But the Berkeley team spent two summers digging and took down about half the cave floor — a solid 650 square feet — more than a meter. If there had been bullets there, they would have found them.

In her books, Theodora Kroeber seized on the similarity of the reported number of dead and the number of burials found and adopted the Kingsley Cave Massacre as part of her Yahi gospel.

She explained away Gore's statement there was no sign of slaughter there with the rather amazing leap of reasoning that even in their depleted state the Yahi must have been able to return and clean up the scene. I shake my head every time I read that.

Every aspect of the tale falls apart with just the slightest scrutiny. Where to start?

Wild Horse Corral is a hollow low in the eastern Tehama County foothills. It's more than 25 miles from Morgan Valley, where Mill Creek turns up toward Lassen Volcanic National Park. Waterman dealt with this problem by changing the name of Cottonwood Creek, a seasonal stream that flows through the hollow, into "Morgan Valley Creek" on a map that accompanies his 1918 paper *The Yana Indians*. Interesting solution.

It's unlikely there were 30-some Indians in the Tehama foothills in 1871. The native population had been systematically moved to reservations since 1859, and comprehensive slaughters were conducted in the area in 1864 and 1866-67.

In 1870 the last of the Yahi tribe had apparently attempted to surrender in an incident called the Five Bows, and they numbered under a dozen.

Even if in 1871 there were 30-some Indians in the Tehama County foothills, knowing the hostility they faced, it's unlikely they would have chosen a place as conspicuous as Kingsley Cave. It's a yawning cavern a dozen-mile walk from the Sacramento Valley floor. It's visible from throughout the mile-wide vale — or "cove" in the nomenclature of the area — into which it opens.

If there were 30-some Indians there, there's no way they could have "cornered" in the cave long enough for three men to kill them all with the weapon technology available in 1871. The cave has no corners. It's shaped like a bandshell, about 75 feet wide and perhaps 25 feet deep at the most. At the first shot, the Indians would have scattered in numerous directions, and there's nothing three men could have done to stop that. They'd have been left shooting at the fleeing people.

And they wouldn't have been shooting rapid-fire by any means. Kingsley's Spencer was an advanced rifle for the time, a repeater with a seven-shot magazine. But after every shot, the trigger guard had to be levered forward to eject the spent shell and then back to set the new charge into the firing chamber. Then the hammer had to be manually cocked before the trigger could be pulled.

I've read accounts that a round could be fired every three or four seconds and mentioned that at a talk I gave years ago at the Tehama County Museum. A man who owns a Spencer came up to me afterward and said there was no way the gun could be fired that rapidly.

The second version of the story

There is another version of the massacre involving Norman Kingsley, and it makes more sense than the common telling of the tale.

However, Eva Marie Apperson's self-published 1971 book *We Knew Ishi* is not well-known, or well-regarded in historical and archaeological circles in Northern California.

That's partly because the woman is openly hostile to the people in those circles at the time she took on writing the book, and for good reason.

She knew she had a good story and approached a history professor at then-Chico State College with the hope he would write it. Instead, she was treated rudely by the professor.

After the rebuff, Apperson decided to write on her own. She communicated with UC Berkeley seeking photographs and access to artifacts collected when her brother-in-law Merle Apperson led Waterman, Alfred Kroeber, Ishi and their group into Yahi country in 1914. Her communication was ignored. When she learned Theodora Kroeber was then starting work on her Ishi books, she took UC Berkeley's failure to respond as an effort to stifle any competition.

And finally, there was a confrontation in the hills of Tehama County when Martin Baumhoff's UC excavation was going on. She wrote that few of the locals came upon a broken-down truck. The college students with the vehicle were evasive about what they were doing, which turned out to be hauling a bunch of human bones that had been dug up at Kingsley Cave.

Her account captures the sensitivity of the people in eastern Tehama County to the native people they'd come to regard as their own. "We Knew Ishi," Apperson wrote, and here were a bunch of grave robbers from the city, surreptitiously hauling a bunch of their neighbors' bones out of the hills.

But even at that, Apperson's book is a hard read. It rambles, pinballs even, with tidbits of information obscured by the writing of someone with passion rather than skill. She was right to seek a professional writer, but I'm glad she didn't just drop the book. I love it, but it's a hard plow to get through.

One of those tidbits is her account of the massacre Norman Kingsley was involved in. She uses the confrontation with the Berkeley students as a stepping off point for her narrative, with the cowboys telling the college boys they'd never heard of a massacre at Kingsley Cave in April 1871.

Instead, they said, that massacre had happened in the late summer of 1865, farther up in the foothills. The story has similarities to Kingsley's purported account. And tellingly, the tactics used are very similar to those used in the attack at the Three Knolls.

Significantly, one of the participants in the killings was W.J. Segraves. He was the one who told Thomas Waterman he had counted 40 to 45 skeletons on the ground after returning to the killing ground a few years later.

It's my belief that Segraves described the attack misplaced at Kingsley Cave to Waterman (who called Segraves one of his most reliable sources), and Waterman assumed that with the similarity in tactics and the year it occurred, that Segraves was describing the Three Knolls.

Segraves is probably the one who placed the attack upstream in Mill Creek Canyon from Black Rock, which is where it would have happened in Apperson's account.

The story's beginning is similar, with a number of close misses that could easily trip up a casual researcher.

In the "gathering season" of 1865 (which is fall), Apperson has "Henry Sill, a Mr. Baker, W.J Segraves, Scott Wellman, the Bogard brothers, Norman Kingsley, Capt. Breckingridge and their cowboys," collecting cattle that had spent the summer in Morgan Valley.

They were bringing their herds together, Apperson wrote, at a place called Dead Horse.

Dead Horse probably refers to a terrace on the west slope of Turner Mountain, southwest of the current town of Mineral. Named for a steep grade on the Tehama Wagon Road, the area includes features called Dead Horse Springs and Dead Horse Falls. It's about 15 miles farther into the hills than Wild Horse Corral. It's not in the Morgan Valley, but it's the kind of place you might gather cattle that had summered there.

It's worth mention that Apperson's account has far more people involved — eight named ranchers and their cowboys. It's a force large enough to have inflicted the kind of bloodshed

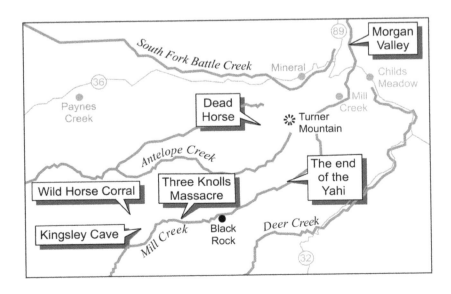

Aerial view looking north toward Lassen Peak on the horizon, shows the gap in the Mill Creek Rim that allowed Yahi to harvest cattle from above the canyon, but which also allowed cattlemen deadly access to the last Yahi village.

attributed to the three riflemen at Kingsley Cave.

As in Waterman's version of Kingsley's tale, Apperson's begins with the finding of a crudely butchered beeve, chunked and with the hide ripped off, and a trail of blood leading away. The roundup is suspended and the group (which had lost other animals that year) heads off in pursuit. The trail leads them into a "deep canyon." Apperson doesn't name the canyon at this point of the narrative, but she mentions elsewhere that it was Mill Creek Canyon.

Significantly, the sheer, high cliffs along the north side of Mill Creek Canyon — the Mill Creek Rim — break for a stretch right on a line between Dead Horse and the place where Waterman mapped the Three Knolls Massacre, upstream from Black Rock. A couple of small small creeks running down from the flats above the canyon have opened a gap in the cliffs providing access that is steep, but not as precipitous as elsewhere.

Apperson writes that the ranchers and their cowboys made their way down into the canyon, and as at the Three Knolls, stopped for the night. Before dawn, they spread out into the same semicircle as was used at the Three Knolls and crept down on the sleeping Indian village.

In yet another similarity to the Three Knolls, the first shot is fired at an Indian who had wakened early and was crossing a creek, making his way downstream along Mill Creek.

As he was crossing one of the small side creeks that flow into the main stream, one of the raiders, thinking he was discovered, shot and killed the Indian, starting the bloodshed.

The canyon here is steeper than down by the Three Knolls, and escape was more difficult. The descriptions attributed to the Three Knolls of men and women leaping into the stream to escape and being shot as they floated downstream make a bit more sense here.

And finally, in the sweep of the grounds that follows the initial slaughter, Norman Kingsley's quote comes into play. He and a few others find a cave close by the village, with the same ton of meat, and a few women and children hiding from the carnage. They are killed, with Kingsley making the switch from his rifle to his pistol at that point.

All in all, it's a far more coherent story than that we have heard all these years set at Kingsley Cave. It actually could have happened the way Apperson describes it. The Kingsley Cave Massacre could not have.

It's also an account that resolves the discrepancies concerning the Three Knolls Massacre. The similarities in tactics and close timing between the two attacks make entangling the two incidents plausible:

• There's a problem with the death toll at the Three Knolls. Apperson's version solves that.

• There's a problem with Sandy Young's description of the Three Knolls as a place hit by a cyclone — likely a village — when it was just a temporary camp on a sandbar. Apperson's version solves that.

• It matches the location Waterman mapped for the Three Knolls.

In short, it resolves all the problems with the stories of both the Three Knolls and Kingsley Cave.

Mariah

Another story has been published that may include an account of an attack in 1865, with the perspective of one of the people who was facing the muzzles of the attackers.

It's the story of a young Maidu woman who was abducted by the Yahi, and who escaped during an attack on her captors. The conventional wisdom is that she escaped during the Three Knolls attack, as that was the conclusion of Sim Moak, who first published the story in his *The Last of the Mill Creeks*, though it was not included in the bobtailed version of Moak's memoir that was published in *Ishi the Last Yahi*. However another, more detailed version of the tale is included in Marie Potts' book *The Northern Maidu*. The captive was Potts' grandmother.

Potts wrote that her grandmother Mariah lived in Big Meadows, which is now largely flooded by Lake Almanor. There was fairly regular conflict between the Big Meadows Maidu and the "Mill Creeks," which in this case may well refer to the Yahi. The Yahi summer range in the meadows high up Deer Creek and Mill Creek was a few short miles from Big Meadows, through terrain that provides few real barriers to travel, or raiding.

Further, the Yahi's closest source of obsidian for arrowheads and other tools were a couple of quarries on Warner Mountain, northwest of modern-day Chester, a short trek into Maidu country. The Yahi had a reason to cross into their neighbors' domain and had never shown a shyness about getting into a fight.

As Potts tells the tale, Mariah was cooking for a crew working on the Humboldt Road. A celebration was planned in Chico on the Fourth of July, and the road crew, along with a number of Maidu men, went to the party. She was alone in the road camp when the Yahi came visiting and carried her away.

The Yahi had a use for Maidu women: as breeding stock. The Yahi needed as many women of childbearing age as possible to replace the losses suffered in the conflict with the settlers in the valley.

Mariah was taken in as a maid to the chief's wife.

The band was very conscious of their peril, according to Potts' recounting of her grandmother's tale. They had set up an early warning system and spent a lot of time practicing what they would do in the event of an attack from the whites. Mariah's job was to pick up the chief's two children and carry them away from danger.

Time went by, and sure enough, the whites did launch an attack. The chief's wife, forgetting the plan, grabbed her children herself, and ran off, leaving Mariah on her own devices. The girl lagged behind, and then took shelter in a cave in a creek bank that she had discovered a short time earlier.

"She stayed hidden during the horrible shooting and killing," Potts wrote, "and, after a couple of days, headed for home." Potts goes on to say it took Mariah several days to find the road camp, but that by late September, "apple-picking time in the white men's orchards," she was home.

That would put the attack on the village in mid-September. But mid-September of what year?

Potts said the drama began in "the summer of 1863, I think it was."

She also said that after the attack, the distinctive footprints of a Mill Creek raider were no longer seen, meaning presumably he was killed. In his book, Robert Anderson also mentioned that the tracks of the same Indian stopped appearing, but only after the Three Knolls attack in 1865.

The whites called the Indian "Big Foot," because his feet were unusually large. He had six toes, which made the tracks distinctive. Potts' description of the tracks is identical. It's interesting that the child who survived the Three Knolls, who Hi Good took a fancy to, also had six toes on her feet.   '

In Moak's version, the abduction happened in the summer of 1864, and the woman escaped "during the fight we had with the Mill Creek," which is clearly a reference to the Three Knolls.

It should be noted Moak called the woman Phoebe. Potts wrote years later that Phoebe was the first wife of Big Meadows Bill. After she died, her sister Mariah became his wife, and Mariah's history became Phoebe's in the minds of many.

The newspapers offer no accounts of conflict between the Mill Creeks and Big Meadows Maidu in 1863, 1864 or 1865. It's unlikely, however, that Mariah would have been at the Three Knolls, if Potts' account is trustworthy.

Mariah got home in late September, more than a month after the Three Knolls. That's a fairly leisurely stroll through the hills. However, an attack by ranchers gathering range cattle could very well have happened in mid-September, about right for Mariah/Phoebe's return home.

Anderson reported that the Mill Creeks had raided the Big Meadows in the days just before they hit Concow Valley in 1865. It seems unlikely that the same band could have conducted both attacks.

There is no confirmation of the "Mill Creek's" attacks in newspaper accounts, although as we have said, that really doesn't mean a thing. However there is an account in the *Oroville Record* of Sept. 23, 1865, that seems to relate to the Mariah/Phoebe tale, and gives it a firm date. The Kingsley massacre and the Three Knolls massacre are entangled — for reasons discussed above — but this does appear to be a time-certain anchor.

"We understand that information has been obtained from an Indian mahala. who escaped to Big Meadows, that but five Indians committed the murder, robbery, and caused the destruction of property at Concow Valley. They made the trip from Mill Creek in five days. The stolen property, money, watches and jewelry was buried in the ground floor of the cave at the time they were attacked by the party of whites in pursuit. Several of the Indians who made their escape from the cave returned two days afterward and dug up the treasure and carried it off. It is also stated the party consisted of 16 bucks, eight of whom were killed and eight escaped."

The real obvious internal contradiction in this is that five conducted the Concow raid, but 16 men were involved somehow. The issue of the cave is problematic, as there are no caves in the immediate vicinity of where I believe the Three Knolls occurred. The cave at the misplaced massacre is well recorded however.

The account suggests the raiders may have been Yahi, although why they would carry off "money, watches and jewelry" to a wilderness where such things have no value is questionable.

I have no proof. I just have a solution that solves all the problems.

The marker for Norman Kingsley's grave, carved on the back of the ornate monument to his more prominent brother George, in the Oak Hill Cemetery in Red Bluff. George Kingsley died three years before Norman Kingsley.

Norman Kingsley's fate

Norman Kingsley reportedly descended into dementia shortly after the attack on the last Yahi village.

The account of dementia is included in a series of 1962 interviews with former Tehama County school trustee Leo Adrian McCoy that are preserved in Judge Herbert South Gans' scrapbook in the Tehama County Library in Red Bluff.

McCoy said Kingsley's dementia increased over time and eventually he "was never seen again until his funeral. He died Aug. 14, 1893, and was buried above his brother in a plot in the old Masonic portion of the Oak Hill Cemetery."

His brother George Kingsley had died in 1890. His ornate grave monument features a carved stone relief of a man flanked by two rifles, a deer and other things. George Kingsley was famous as a hunter.

George Kingsley operated a glove factory and was a leading citizen of Red Bluff. A renowned hunter, he was frequently mentioned in glowing terms in the *Red Bluff Independent* newspaper.

That could be linked with an intriguing little item from the Feb. 13, 1867, edition of the *Independent* under the headline "Insane":

"Deputy Sheriff Brown took departure for Stockton on the boat yesterday having in charge an insane man, the brother of one of our leading citizens. We withhold his name in case he should ever be cured. In such a case the public record of his insanity would remain as a cloud on his prospects in life."

Since the newspaper in previous issues had been willing to name those sent to the sanatorium in Stockton, the deletion of the name here is curious. One can wonder if the brother was George Kingsley and the newspaper's fondness for him led to the change in policy.

However, I found an article from the *Sacramento Union* in September 1882 that Norman Kingsley had killed a 700-pound bear up in Tehama County on the 17th of that month.

The newspapers back then would pick up items from one another pretty much verbatim, so I have to assume the *Union* got that from one of the Red Bluff papers. I can't see them mistaking Norman for George.

Unfortunately I can't check because of the gap in the Red Bluff paper microfilms mentioned in Chapter 9 that includes 1882.

However since George was the famed hunter, that adds more credence to the possibility it was he who killed the bear.

Chapter 16

The Campo Seco bluff in Dye Creek Canyon, a few miles east of the Sacramento Valley. A cave in the bluff's southside was the site of a massacre of Indians, probably in 1866.

1866–67

Most of the streams flowing out of the eastern Tehama County foothills issue from narrow gorges that offer little glimpse of what is upstream. But Dye Creek is different. A bluff a couple of miles upstream from the canyon floor is visible and looks like the bow of a massive ship, spreading the canyon gates like a wake.

The bluff is the Campo Seco, perhaps the most impressive bit of nature's sculpture in a country where extreme landscapes are commonplace. The south face is a sheer cliff, 60 to 80 feet high. The bluff's base is pockmarked with caves that show signs of Yahi occupation.

But a mile or two upstream, there's a cave that's different. It hangs beneath a sloping out-cropping extending from the bluff. A narrow ledge leads up to the cave, and beyond, up to the bluff's top.

The cave offers a clear view down the canyon. Anyone taking shelter there could see trouble coming in that direction from a long way off, in plenty of time to escape up the trail to the top of the bluff.

But raiders coming from upstream or from the bluff above would turn the cave into a trap, at a place that would leave anyone in the cave no escape except a sprint down that narrow ledge along the cliff face.

The author's wife Laura at the base of the Campo Seco bluff. The sheer cliffs provided sanctuary, but were also a deadly trap.

It looks like that's what happened. That cliff face is pock-marked, possibly from gunfire directed toward it. A large, soft lead bullet like those in use in the 1860s was found at the base of the cliff face in the 1980s. And downhill from the cave, a survey a few years earlier by Sacramento State University archaeologists found a skull that had rolled under a rock.

That slope was littered with skulls about 90 years earlier, according to a witness quoted by Thomas Waterman in his 1918 publication, *The Yana Indians*. He quoted Frank Norvell as saying he counted 33 skulls when he came upon the scene while herding sheep there in 1869.

The number is highly suspect. Norvell was 16 at the time, and more than 40 years passed between the teenager's seeing and the adult's telling. The cave also isn't large enough to hold that many people, and it's unlikely there were enough Indians left in the area at that time for 33 to gather in one place

The site is unique along the Sacramento Valley's eastern slope that it's the only one where the land shows actual physical evidence of a massacre. And yet while the location is clear, the time when the killings happened and those responsible are more vague, a flip on the usual situation.

The killings may have been those in 1864 that were located in a cave, involving either gunfire or strychnine, as described in a previous chapter. They could have been the work of a group of raiders coming north out of Butte County in 1866, in response to a theft. Or more likely, the killings were done by a group coming south from Shasta County later that year after a white woman was killed there.

Anderson and the Moaks

Death may have come to Campo Seco in April, following an Indian raid east and north of Chico. The house of Albert Silva on Little Chico Creek and a couple of homes on Mud Creek were sacked by a group of 12 Indians. Some shots were fired at Silva's wife and a hired hand, without any effect except to scare them away, which seemed to be the point.

Silva's neighbors included Sim and Jake Moak, who had a history of hunting the Indians. They gathered up a few neighbors, picked up some crackers and bacon in Chico, and moved north to the Rock Creek home of Robert Anderson, who was also well known for killing Indians.

They added on a few of Anderson's Rock Creek neighbors and headed north to Deer Creek Flat, a bluff just south of Deer Creek. Crossing the creek, they climbed a bluff and found an Indian encampment atop it.

A running battle ensued, with at least three Indians killed, one after hiding behind a waterfall down a ravine, according to Anderson.

And then there was this, in a May 21, 1866, letter from Levi Moak to his sister:

"Jake wounded a squaw and she hid in the brush. He found her and she came at him. He shot her through and the blood spouted over his pants. The papoose she had strapped to her and the ball had broke its leg, so he put it out of its misery with his pistol.

"I think they will begin to learn not to come on Little Chico to rob any more for every time of late they have got the worst of it," he concluded.

Anderson apparently returned from the raid wearing Mrs. Silva's flowered hat, with the scalps of killed Indians hanging from the back of his mule.

Eva Marie Apperson in *We Knew Ishi* puts this attack on the Campo Seco and calls it the last battle with the Mill Creeks. But by my reading it actually happened on Digger Pine Flat, a bluff on the south side of Deer Creek about 10 miles southeast of the Dye Creek prominence.

Anderson, in his book *Fighting the Mill Creeks*, puts the incident in 1863, but Levi Moak's 1866 letter gives a date around April 24 of that year. That's clearly a more accurate date than Anderson's, whose book was written 40 years after the fact.

The Moak letter was one of those lost when the Camp Fire destroyed the Gold Nugget Museum in Paradise in November 2018.

The Dersch killing

A larger splurge of killing followed the Aug. 22, 1866, killing of a white woman in Shasta County. Anna Marie Dersch was shot by a couple of Indians while making soap at her home at the Bear Creek crossing of what's now called Dersch Road. The site's about six miles east of modern-day Anderson.

It does not appear to have been a killing of opportunity, differing from the others during the Mill Creek War. Rather it was retribution for the beating of three Indians by a tenant of the Dersches a few years earlier, according to local tradition and a plaque at the site.

A party of six formed to pursue the Indians after the killing. The *Red Bluff Independent* newspaper reported they followed a long trail, crossing and recrossing the Sacramento River and heading well into the hills and back before losing the trail.

The paper reported the war party camped the night of Aug. 28 at the head of Antelope Creek. The following day they moved south about eight miles and stumbled upon a camp of eight Indians.

"Blue smoke curled up from the alders and the sharp crack of rifles told that the poor woman so foully murdered, was being fearfully avenged," the *Independent* reported, in the oft-overwrought

Plaque at the site of the Dersch homestead, east of Anderson in Shasta County.

journalism of the age.

Four Indians — two men and two women — were killed outright and three were wounded but limped off. Items stolen from the Dersch home were reportedly found.

The raiders withdrew to the Antelope Creek flour mill, where they were fed and feted. Returning the next day they found the four bodies had been burned, along with a fifth who had apparently been able to move some distance before dying. A blood trail showed he was dragged back and added to the pyre.

Was this the Campo Seco killing?

It's possible. The plaque at the Dersch site says the posse formed after the killing had pursued and "killed most of the Indians at their Dye Creek Camp." These historical plaques can make no claim to accuracy but are based on local tradition that may be more trustworthy than the ramblings of historians, myself included.

The account in the *Independent* that the raiders moved south eight miles from Antelope Creek could have put them in the vicinity of Dye Creek. And it reported the war party had to change course when they suddenly "came upon a high palisade of rocks." That's a pretty good description of the Campo Seco.

But the mention of alders is a problem. It's a creekside tree that is missing up against the bluff where the cave is located. The Antelope Creek flour mill was also farther than two miles from the Campo Seco, the distance included in the Independent account.

The record of the next few months provides a number of alternatives with claims to the Campo Seco slaughter.

The final solution

Adjacent to the column in the Sept. 5, 1866, edition of the *Red Bluff Independent* that records the response to the killing of Mrs. Dersch is another story. It calls for contributions to purchase state-of-the-art weapons for the raiders in the hills, and to fund a bounty for the Indian scalps they might bring in. Funds were also raised in Shasta County.

A party of seven was organized near Millville in southern Shasta County. It was provisioned and armed with Henry rifles and spent the next several months hunting down and killing pretty much any Indians they found.

War parties were also sent from Chico and Trinity County but returned after a short time without success.

The Millville seven continued with their business, however.

The *Shasta Courier* on Oct. 6 reported the killing of four or five Indians in a cave "on the head of Antelope Creek," which might be the Campo Seco killings.

About that same time, a rancheria of Indian laborers on a ranch on the valley floor was attacked. The *Red Bluff Independent* reported Oct. 10 that the previous week, property stolen from the Dersch home was found on the Gerke grant, *"and the work of vengeance and slaughter commenced."*

The Gerke grant is the property near Vina first settled by Peter Lassen. Several hundred acres of it are now the Abbey of New Clairvaux.

The *Independent* doesn't give a death toll, but it defends the killings — *"It cannot be helped, and it must be done"* — with a remarkably racist rant that a white man's life is worth that of a hundred Indians, as long as the white man doesn't live with the Indians. *"In that case, the [Indian] is the best man of the two."*

On Oct. 19, the *Independent* reported meeting with John Boyce, captain on the Millville raiders, who was in Red Bluff to raise funds to continue the campaign.

He was asked how it was going. *"A strange smile lighted up the features of this lonely man, bereft of all he loved on earth by the hands of the murdering savages, as he answered, 'Well, we have planted a few of them and keep pretty steady to work.'"*

Boyce was the brother of a woman who'd been killed by Indians two years earlier.

The killings continued into 1867. Five were killed on Bucks Flat up Little Antelope Creek. Seven were killed on Inks Creek.

But ultimately, the Indian hunters ran out of people to kill, and the Mill Creek War fizzled to an end.

Chapter 17

Author's wife Laura beside a penstock at the presumed site of the Occidental Mine in Deer Creek Canyon. Thomas Waterman wrote that the Yahi stole a bag of supplies from the site in 1906, when theft had become critical to the few survivors as their traditional ways of life became more difficult.

Delaying the inevitable

As the spring of 1867 turned to summer, the organized carnage inflicted on the Indians in eastern Tehama, Butte and Shasta counties ended.

About 15 white people had been killed in six years of the Mill Creek War. The Indian death toll is harder to estimate, but it's in the hundreds. It's certainly over a thousand if you add in those who died of malaria in 1863 at the camp on John Bidwell's ranch in Chico, and on the forced march from there to Nome Cult.

Almost all the Yana and the Yahi had been killed. Large numbers of the Wintun in Shasta and Tehama counties had been killed. Dozens of Maidu in Butte County had been killed. Hundreds more from all those tribes had been forcibly removed from the lands where they had lived for thousands of years.

We know the names of almost all of the whites who died but none of the Indians, unless you're willing to regard "Chief Codfish," lynched in 1863 in Butte Creek Canyon, as a true name.

By 1867, the surviving Yahi had taken to mastering the art of hiding, although there were still unpleasant encounters with their new neighbors.

For instance, a chain of incidents in 1870 was recounted by Thomas Waterman in his *The Yana Indians.*

W.J. Segraves told Waterman that in March of that year he lost some cattle, apparently to Indians. He recruited Hi Good and two others to pursue the raiders.

They found an empty Yahi village on Mill Creek — with the remains of the butchered beef — and pressed on. Seeing a band of about 15 approaching, they set an ambush. Most of the Yahi broke off before coming into gunfire range, but an "Old Doctor" was shot and killed, and two women and a young girl were captured.

Two weeks later, five men and seven women turned up at Segraves' cabin. The men ritually offered their five bows in an apparent attempt to surrender and be taken to the reservation, as the tribe had attempted to do in 1860 at Black Rock.

Segraves, uncertain what to do, took them to Good's sheep camp in Acorn Hollow. Good was away at the time, and the Yahi and Good's crew awaited his return. One of the herders threw a rope over a branch to weigh himself. The Yahi, taking that to mean they would be hanged, bolted into the brush.

A few months later, on May 1, Good was killed by "Indian Ned," who worked for him. Ned was subsequently killed by Good's friend Sandy Young.

The encounters would continue, according to Waterman. Two Yahi women were "lassoed" in 1878 at Black Oak Grove, and a man and child were wounded. The women were taken to the reservation.

As the Yahi became more proficient at hiding, the encounters dwindled. Occasionally someone roaming the foothills would have an arrow shot at him from an unseen archer. Tools and possessions of the hidden people would be found and carried off.

But the incidents were not sensational, not the kind of thing that would capture the attention of the outside world. And the history of the Yahi faded to a clean slate for the eventual promotion of the Ishi myths.

However, the newcomers who began building herding and hunting cabins in Yahi country clearly knew the tribe was still there. That was because the Indians regularly raided those cabins and the gardens around them for food.

The Yahi became as proficient at theft as at hiding, and it was becoming a more and more important part of their survival strategy. It was a necessary change because the newcomers' infringement restricted access to traditional sources of food and other essentials the Indians had gathered from the natural world for centuries. They replaced those natural sources with human-made sources as they had no choice.

The take at times was large. There's a report of the meat of 10 hogs weighing 200 pounds each being taken after butchering. Fruit trees and vegetable gardens were stripped when residents were away or sleeping. Foodstuffs, clothing and more was stolen from empty cabins, with the raiders leaving nary a trace of their visit.

Most of those who were robbed seemed to have regarded it as the price of doing business — rent, as it were -- for living in Yahi country.

An exception might have been Elijah Graham, a homesteader on Deer Creek. After one too many robberies, he was reputed to have poisoned either a sack of flour or a bottle of whisky — depending on the storyteller — and marked it clearly as poisoned.

His reasoning was that Indians wouldn't have been able to read the words, and would eat or drink and die. He must have presumed that white folks had 100 percent literacy in those days.

There were other encounters, where someone would stumble upon a hidden Indian, and have an arrow or two shot at them. The archer would flee, sometimes leaving behind things like arrow- making kits.

And then there were accounts of the Speegle children swimming in Deer Creek near its junction with Sulphur Creek, having stones falling into the water from the rocks above. It was no threat and was understood to be an advisory that it was time to yield the stream to the Yahi for fishing or collecting water.

The situation changed in early November of 1908, when some surveyors doing the legwork for a proposed dam on Deer Creek encountered a naked Indian fishing with a spear on a rock in the middle of the stream.

He was apparently the man who would later be given the name of Ishi.

He snarled at them, and they fled to their base at Apperson's Cow Camp, just a bit upstream.

The surveyors' story prompted Jack Apperson to go look for the Indian camp the following day. He found a hidden trail up the bluff from where the Indian had been seen and followed it until an arrow was fired in his direction, narrowly missing his head.

He retreated, but as the day's surveying continued, the party began to make out human shapes through the dense brush that had concealed the last village of the Yahi.

As they broke into the sanctuary, several people fled. An old woman with injured legs was found rolled up in a blanket. She was given water and left alone, probably with the expectation she would die.

The camp showed that the Yahi were no longer the Yahi who had lived in that land for centuries. There were still traditional things like a stone metate. But at a spot where someone had knapped arrowheads for years, the debitage was bottle glass, rather than the basalt or obsidian used before the newcomers arrived.

There was a well of sorts, a pit dug down into the high water table of the ledge that would fill with water for part of the year, eliminating the need to make the risky trek down to the creek.[1]

The three structures in the camp were built with wood that had been cut with a saw stolen from one of the cabins in the area. A canvas tarp provided the roof for one.

There were numerous metal containers for water and other liquids, and pots and pans. The old woman was given water from a full canteen found near her.[2]

The ranchers who were working with the surveyors took a number of items from the camp, as a kind of payback from the years of theft they had experienced.

The group returned to their base for dinner and came back to find the old woman gone.

The discovery of the camp created a brief sensation in the press and also drew Waterman up for a visit in 1910 to record what was there.

But the "Last Wild Indians in North America" had vanished, and the public's fickle attention drifted elsewhere.

NOTES

1. Thomas Waterman, in his *The Yana Indians*, suggested this pit was packed with snow in winter for use during the spring. But the site, at about 1,500-foot elevation, doesn't get much snow, none in most years.

2. When the camp was rediscovered in 1991, for the first time since Ishi had taken the anthropologists there in 1914, a number of Log Cabin Maple Syrup cans were found. This makes perfect sense if you've ever tasted acorn soup, which can be bitter even after the tannic acid has been leached out of it.

Chapter 18

Photo from the 1990s shows the author's wife Laura beside an old grain swather at the Savercool Place on Mill Creek, upstream from Black Rock.

Lost in the discussion

A bit upstream from Black Rock on Mill Creek, there's a spot marked on Geological Survey maps as the Savercool Place.

It stays green much of the year due to a seep from the bluffs above. It's largely overgrown by blackberries today, but it's clear some settlers tried to make a go of it there many years ago. There are ancient apple trees, surrounded by masses of bear poop. There's an old grain swather, rusting away.

It was quite a bustling place once, with a telephone and a turbine in the creek to generate electricity, according to Beverly Benner Ogle's *Spirits of Black Rock*. Ogle grew up on a ranch just downstream from Black Rock.

The Benner ranch is still there, but the Savercools' effort failed after just a few decades.

However, on the same flat as the Savercool Place, there's a Yahi village site that was excavated by Lassen National Forest archaeologists in the 1990s. The artifacts found indicated the spot was used seasonally for a span of at least 1,500 years. That was quite a bit longer than the Savercools survived.

The maps of Yahi Country are marked with many such sites bearing only the names of newcomers, rather than the names the Yahi might have given them. Visit those locations and you will find the rusted metal of the newcomers, while the artifacts left by the Yahi are subtle enough to be invisible.

And this is the pattern throughout America. We have built cities, factories, farms, highways and what not, upon the bones of the First Peoples.

Our creations have provided livelihoods that allowed us to ignore those who came before us, and distractions that have allowed us to forget them.

Many of us don't know whose land we occupy, and most of us don't know how those people lived. And most of us just don't care.

Instead we have relied on personal mythologies to imagine the past. Generally, that mythology has been shaped by history colored by fiction, about noble pioneers subduing heathen Indians to allow progress to spread from the Atlantic to the Pacific. It was our Manifest Destiny. We were on a mission from god to conquer North America for civilization.

Most of us read that American Indians were howling savages, circling wagon trains, raping women, killing and mutilating men, and kidnapping children. There's no question that that happened, but the other side of the story was never told.

We never heard about slaughters like the Wounded Knee massacre, which would have done Hitler proud. If you'd known the facts you might have concluded that Custer had it coming at the Little Bighorn due to what he'd done at Washita River. Others learned that scalping may have been introduced to the Americas by Europeans. And at Sand Creek, we learned the Colorado vigilantes had gouged the vaginas out of the Indian women they'd killed, and stretched them over their saddle pommels to make purses, as they rode back to Denver.

But as it is said, the winners write the history. And what we wrote is that we were doing god's will. That complicates any effort to actually appreciate how the Yahi lived.

Yahi country is incredibly harsh. It stretches across two very different environments. The upper meadows are lush from late spring to late fall, but they are blanketed with snow in the times between. The lower canyons could support the tribe in winter and early spring, but baked white and barren before summer settled in.

It's remarkable that the tribe could find a way to survive the challenge of their homeland. But they did it for thousands of years. It's a remarkable story that became irrelevant when Ishi came out of the hills.

He became a rock star Indian. The last Stone Age Indian in North America. The last wild Indian in North America. Quickly, the "Mill Creek" myth was entangled with Ishi, and he became the last survivor of a tribe that had terrorized Northern California for years.

It made Manifest Destiny just so much sweeter. The Yahi stopped being a few hundred Indians surviving the challenges of their land. Instead, the Yahi became a band of bloodthirsty savages spreading terror. And now, the last of that tribe had staggered into Oroville, starving and broken. Manifest Destiny had won.

But Ishi was not starving. Looking back, it's peculiar to think how we might have come to conclude that a man who'd lived his whole life in the hills might have forgotten how to eat.

And Ishi hadn't staggered into Oroville as a broken man. Ad Kessler, who'd gathered Ishi into custody in the slaughterhouse east of Oroville, told about tracking Ishi back, and finding the widely spread footprints of a man who was running hard into Oroville, as if from something he feared.

What he was fleeing may have been captured by the Maidu artist Frank Day, who created a painting called "Ishi and Companion at Iam Mool."

Iam Mool is the point where the forks of the Feather River come together, now submerged beneath Lake Oroville.

Day said he and his father had come upon Ishi there, the day before he turned up in Oroville. Ishi was treating a man with a gunshot wound. Ishi's hair was still long them, but he'd burned it off by the following day when he was "captured" in Oroville.

There are a number of indications that Ishi was an Indian "doctor." And Indian doctors could be killed by the survivors of patients who died. It sounds like Ishi lost his final patient, and ran for his life into Oroville.

But the circumstance of his arrival in Oroville didn't matter. The last wild Indian had surrendered to the dominant culture.

He became a living display at the University of California's San Fransisco anthropology museum, knapping arrowheads for tourists and answering endless questions from the professors seeking insight to a culture we had destroyed.

And when he died, he was dissected like a lab animal. His brain was cut out and sent to the Smithsonian. The rest of his body was cremated and placed in a small urn, put on display at the Mount Olivet Cemetery in Colma, south of San Fransisco.

Today there are ranches and cabins and resorts in the Yahi high meadows. There's the Benner Ranch and a number of hunting or herding cabins in the tribe's winter range. But they all rely on supplies carried in on gasoline-powered wheels. No one lives there strictly on what the land provides, something the Yahi managed for eons.

To a degree it's understandable. The salmon runs have been decimated. Privately owned cattle have displaced the deer that belonged to all. And the idea of using fire to manage the vegetation appalls many city dwellers, whose votes overwhelm so many things that rural residents understand to be important..

People talk about how amazing it was that the last

The urn in which Ishi's ashes -- except for his brain -- were placed in the Mount Olivet Cemetery in Coloma, south of San Francisco.

remnant of the Yahi were able to stay hidden. But what's surprising to me is that a people were able live there at all for so many hundreds of years. That the Yahi survived in a country so harsh seems to me to be worth acknowledging.

It is a remarkable accomplishment for a people to have survived for centuries in a country as harsh as any I've encountered.

It is an affirmation that the history of the Yahi is worthy of the kinds of attention the Sioux and the Comanche attract, even though the Yahi were just a few hundred strong, living a lifestyle that had been abandoned by the thousands of Indians who had set down roots in the Sacramento Valley.

When Theodora Kroeber's books came out, the Ishi myth took another turn. The Yahi became the first ecologists, living in harmony with nature, although in reality, they shaped it dramatically with fire.

Kroeber painted the sympathetic picture of a group of people living as they had for centuries, only to be exterminated when they got in the way.

In the grand scheme of things, Theodora Kroeber's books, flawed though they are, may be more valuable than what I have written here. Hers were the first books to awaken thousands of people to the things that were done to the American Indians, rather than focusing on the things Indians did to newcomers.

But after Kroeber's books came out, minds were opened. Those personal mythologies — so important to how we live our lives as they guide our actions — began to shift to recognize what was done to the First Peoples.

Incidents that had been de-emphasized because they so were inexcusable found a place in the personal mythologies of more and more people.

Kroeber opened a Pandora's box, forcing us to look at our actions from the perspective of another, even though with the Yahi, there is no "another" left.

The enlightenment isn't universal. After Ishi's brain was reunited with his ashes and they were buried in his homeland, a monument to him was erected at The Narrows on the Lassen Trail.

Shortly after it was completed, some idiot fired a number of bullets into the brass, necessitating repairs.

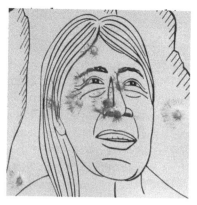

The Ishi monument at the Narrows on the Lassen Trail. Shortly after this monument was built, someone fired a number of bullets into it.

me "she was an Indian before it was cool to be an Indian." She also told me of the abuse she had suffered as a "prairie nigger."

This came as she was teaching me about basketweaving, and how the weavers cared for the plants they needed. She disproved the idea that Indians didn't have agriculture. It just wasn't an agriculture that we newcomers could understand. Or perhaps, we didn't want to understand.

Even now, the preconceptions and the stereotypes are hard to shed.

When a Northern California tourism advocate learned I was writing this book, she urged me to create a visitor guide to the Ishi Wilderness. I told her if you tried to make it a destination, people attracted would die. It's that harsh a place.

The roads in are dirt, narrow and steep, and not maintained. Sharp rocks on the roadway are likely to give you a flat tire or two. There's often a long, fatal drop off one side of the road, in lieu of a shoulder. And once you're in, if something goes wrong, that's it. Help cannot be summoned.

And the country is haunted. By maleficent spirits.

As I mentioned earlier, my wife and I backpacked in 1995 from the Sacramento Valley floor near Red Bluff to Childs Meadow, in a bid to replicate the Yahi annual migration.

A half-dozen days into the hike, the backpacking stove didn't work one morning, and the instant coffee that was so critical to our progress was missing. Anyone who has taken a long hike like that will tell how important instant coffee is.

We hiked on and came to a sandy beach at the mouth of the gulch where the massacre misidentified as the Three Knolls would have happened. It was a simple task to build a fire on the beach to allow us to boil water for coffee.

But at that spot, the thought came to me that we were a bit ahead of schedule, and perhaps we could go explore the gulch.

With that thought, the tree leaves above us began to shiver, and the wind picked up to a howl. And a gust of wind came out of the gulch that extinguished my little fire in just an instant.

I've built a lot of fires in my years, and they don't usually get blown out. I reinforced the fire pit framework, reloaded the tinder, and reignited the fire.

And again, the wind rose in the tree branches above the beach, and in a bluster of rustling vegetation and a cloud of leaves, a gust came down that again extinguished the fire.

Hmm.

I'd done this dance before. There were a number of times when Yahi country sought to kill me. And there were times when the landscape volunteered to show me things it thought I needed to know.

And there, on that morning on Mill Creek, the Yahi wanted me to move on. It didn't want me to explore up that gulch where there were 30 or more ghosts, trying to find peace.

I'd become close enough to the Yahi that a warning to back off was recognizable, even though the ghosts spoke in a language I can't understand.

I agreed in my mind to stay out of the gulch, and the

The author trying to build a fire in June 1995 on Mill Creek. The spirits of the Yahi weren't having any of it.

wind gusts relented to allow me to make coffee. We moved on. It was clear we weren't welcome.

You aren't welcome either. This book isn't an invitation to explore Yahi County. It's a warning to stay out.

Instead, the exploration needs to happen within you. You need to understand the things that were done to the California Indians, and to the other First Peoples across the continent. It's important to understand what your predecessors and ours did to those who lived where you and I live now, in order to claim the land for ourselves.

The country you need to explore is in your heart and mind.

About the author

Steve Schoonover is a long-time Chico newsman, having spent about 40 years in the *Chico Enterprise-Record* newsroom in a variety of roles. In the 1990s he became intrigued by the Yahi, and how their history had been warped to support the myths of Ishi. He is now mostly retired and lives in Chico with his wife Laura Urseny, who also worked at the *E-R*.

Bibliography

A primary source for this book is microfilms of Northern California newspapers from the 1850s to the 1870s, including the *Butte Democrat, Butte Record, Chico Courant, Chico Daily Enterprise, Chico Record, Red Bluff Beacon, Red Bluff Independent, Red Bluff People's Cause* and *Shasta Courier*.

Allen, Susan — *The Nome Lackee Indian Reservation. Wagon Wheels*, Colusi County Historical Society, Volume 17, No. 1, Colusa, CA, 1967.

Anderson, Kat — *Native Californians as Ancient and Contemporary Cultivators*. Paper presented at the seventh annual California Indian Conference, Sonoma State University, October 1991. Expanded version published in *Before the Wilderness: Environmental Management by Native Californians*. Ballena Press, Menlo Park, CA, 1993.

Anderson, Robert — *Fighting the Mill Creeks: Being a Personal Accounting of Campaigns Against Indians of the Northern Sierra*. Chico Record Press, Chico, CA, 1909. Included in Ishi the Last Yahi: A Documentary History.

Apperson, Eva Marie — *We knew Ishi*. Self-published (?), Vina, CA, 1971.

Bakker, Elna — *An Island Called California: An Ecological Introduction to its Natural Communities*. University of California Press, Berkeley, Los Angeles, London, 1972.

Baumhoff, Martin A. — *Excavation of Site Teh-1 (Kingsley Cave)*. University of California Archaeological Survey, Berkeley, 1955.

Baumgardner, Frank H. III — *Killing for Land in Early California: Indian Blood at Round Valley, 1856-1863*. Algora Publishing, New York, 2006.

Bidwell, Annie E.K. — *Rancho Chico Indians*. Edited by Dorothy Hill, Bidwell Mansion Association, Chico, CA, 1980.

Blackburn, Thomas C. and Anderson, Kat (editors) — *Before the Wilderness: Environmental Management by Native Californians*. Ballena Press, Menlo Park, CA, 1993. Especially valuable chapters cited elsewhere in this bibliography, but the whole book is a treasure.

Bruff, J. Goldsborough — *Gold Rush: The Journals, Drawings, and Other Papers of J. Goldsborough Bruff, Captain, Washington City and California Mining Association.* Columbia University Press, New York, 1949.

Bryant, Edward — *What I Saw in California.* University of Nebraska Press, 1985. First published by D. Appleton & Co., New York, 1848.

Bungay, Rod — *The Edible Wild Plants of Butte County.* Self-published, Magalia, CA, 1987.

Carson, Thankful A. — *Captured by the Mill Creeks.* Self-published (?), Chico, CA, 1915. Included in Ishi the Last Yahi: A Documentary History.

Chartkoff, Joseph L. and Chartkoff, Kerry Kona — *The Archaeology of California.* Stanford University Press, Menlo Park, CA, 1984.

Clarke, Charlotte Bringle — *Edible and Useful Plants of California.* University of California Press, Berkeley, Los Angeles, 1977.

Cook, Sherburne F. — *The Conflict Between the California Indian and White Civilization.* University of California Press, Berkeley, 1976.

Elasser, A.B — *Notes on Yana Ethnobotany.* Journal of California and Great Basin Anthropology, Malki Museum, Morongo Indian Reservation, Banning, CA, 1981.

Dobbins, Rebecca — *Maidu Artist Frank Day's Vision of Ishi.* Presentation during "Ishi: The Man and His Times, Revisited" symposium at James More Theater Lecture Hall, The Oakland Museum, CA, March 26, 1994. Similar information is included in Dobbins' chapter of same name in Ishi in Three Centuries, edited by Karl and Clifton Kroeber, University of Nebraska Press, Lincoln, 2003.

Gifford, E.W. and Klimek, Stanislaw — *Cultural Element Distributions: II Yana.* University of California Publications in American Archaeology and Ethnology, Berkeley, 1936.

Golla, Victor — *Ishi's Language.* Presentation during "Ishi: The Man and His Times, Revisited" symposium at James More Theater Lecture Hall, The Oakland Museum, CA, March 26, 1994. Similar information is included in Golla's chapter of same name in *Ishi in Three Centuries*, edited by Karl and Clifton Kroeber, University of Nebraska Press, Lincoln and London, 2003.

— Also, personal communication.

Greenway, Gregory B. — *Seasonality and Site Function at Dead Man's Cave (CA-Teh-290)*. Proceedings of the Society for California Archaeology, Volume 17, 2004.

Groot, Cornelis and Margolis, Leo (editors) — *Pacific Salmon Life Histories*. University of British Columbia Press, Vancouver, 1991. Section on Sacramento Valley chinook salmon written by M.C. Healey.

Hamusek-McGann, Blossom — *The Stratigraphy and Archaeology at CA-Teh-1490: A Hunting Camp in Yana Territory, Northern California*. Archaeology Research Program, California State University, Chico, 1988. Prepared for the California Department of Forestry.

—*What X Equals: The Archaeological and Geological Distribution of "Source X" Tuscan Obsidian in Northern California*. Unpublished master's thesis, Department of Anthropology, California State University, Chico, 1993.

Heizer Robert F. and Elasser, Albert B. — *The Natural World of the California Indians*, University of California Press, Berkeley and Los Angeles, 1980.

Heizer, Robert F. (editor) — *The Destruction of the California Indians*. University of Nebraska Press, Lincoln, 1974.

Heizer, Robert F. and Kroeber, Theodora (editors) — *Ishi the Last Yahi: A Documentary History*. University of California Press, Berkeley, and Los Angeles, 1979. Especially valuable chapters cited by author elsewhere in this bibliography.

Hill, Dorothy — *The Indians of Chico Rancheria*. Ka Ca Ma Press, Chico, CA, 1978.

— *Maidu Use of Native Flora and Fauna*. Self-published (?), Chico, CA, 1972.

— Also, personal communication.

Hinton, Leanne — *Flutes of Fire: Essays on California Indian languages*. Heyday Books, Berkeley, CA, 2016

Hinton, Leanne and Susan L. Roth — *Ishi's Tale of Lizard*. Farrar-Straus-Giroux, New York 1995.

Hislop, Donald Leslie — *The Nome Lackee Indian Reservation, 1854-1870*. Occasional publication No. 4 of the Association for Northern California Records and Research, Chico, CA, 1978.

Holliday, J.S. — *The World Rushed In: The California Gold Rush*

Experience. Simon and Schuster, New York, 1981.

Hunt, Ann — *The Allen and Jones Massacres and the Extermination of the Yana*. The Covered Wagon, Shasta Historical Society, Redding, CA, 1960.

Johnson, Jerald J. — *Yana, in Handbook of North American Indians, Volume 8*, California. Smithsonian Institution, 1978.

Johnston, James D. — *Bear's Hiding Place (Wowunupo'me Tetna)*. Unpublished (?) U.S. Forest Service manuscript, 1992.

Kessler, Adolph — *Ishi's First Days in a New World*. Oral history collected by Richard Smith, Feb. 7, 1979. Published in *Conversations with the Past*, Association for Northern California Historical Research, Chico, 2017. Copy of the taped interview in the author's possession.

Kroeber, Alfred L. — *Handbook of the Indians of California*. Dover Publications edition, New York, 1976. Originally published by U.S. Government Printing Office as Bulletin 78 of the Bureau of American Ethnology of the Smithsonian Institution, Washington, D.C., 1925.

Kroeber, Karl and Clifton — *Ishi in Three Centuries* (editors), University of Nebraska Press, Lincoln, 2003. Especially valuable chapters cited by author elsewhere in this bibliography.

Kroeber, Theodora — *Ishi in Two Worlds: A Biography of the Last Wild Indian in North America*. University of California Press, Berkeley and Los Angeles, 1962.

— *Ishi Last of His Tribe*. Parnassus Press, Berkeley, CA, 1964

Lassen National Forest and Mountain Heritage Associates — *Black Rock and Beyond: A Decade of Archaeological Test Excavations in Yahi Territory*. U.S. Forest Service, Susanville, 2001.

Lewis, E.J — *Tehama County, California, Illustrations ... With Historical Sketch of the County*. Elliott & Moore, San Francisco, 1880.

Lewis, Henry T. — *Patterns of Indian Burning in California: Ecology and Ethnohistory*. Originally published as Ballena Press Anthropological Papers 1; reprinted in *Before the Wilderness: Environmental Management by Native Californians*. Ballena Press, Menlo Park, CA, 1993.

Lydon, Phillip A — *Geology and Lahars of the Tuscan Formation*. Geological Society of America, 1968.

Lingenfelter, Keith — *Supervisors of the Nome Lackee Indian*

Reservation. Wagon Wheels, Colusi County Historical Society, Volume 27, No. 1, Colusa, CA, 1977.

Luthin, Herbert and Hinton, Leanne — *The Days of a Life: What Ishi's Stories Can Tell About Ishi.* Chapter in Ishi in Three Centuries, edited by Karl and Clifton Kroeber, University of Nebraska Press, Lincoln, 2003.

Mansfield, George C. — *History of Butte County, California, with Biographical Sketches ...* Historic Record Co., Los Angeles, 1918.

Martin, Charles A. — *The Battle of Eagle Peak: New Perspective on an Old History Mystery. Wagon Wheels,* Colusi County Historical Society, Volume 61, No. 1, Colusa, CA, 2011. Accompanied in the same issue by The Eagle Peak Posse by Gene Russell. Several earlier accounts of the battle occurred in earlier editions of Wagon Wheels.

McGie, Joseph F. — *History of Butte County.* Butte County Board of Education, 1982. Historical Record Company.

Moak, Jacob, Levi and Simeon — Letters written home, copied with permission from the files of the Gold Nugget Museum, Paradise, CA. Originals were later destroyed by the Camp Fire, Nov. 8, 2018.

Moak, Sim — *The Last of the Mill Creeks and Early Life in California.* Self-published (?), Chico, CA, 1923. Excerpts were included in *Ishi the Last Yahi: A Documentary History.*

Nathan, Elroy N. — *A Historical Geography of Cohasset Ridge.* Unpublished thesis, California State University, Chico, 1966.

Neasham, Ernest R. — *Fall River Valley: An Examination of Historical Sources.* The Citadel Press, Sacramento, CA, 1857.

Perry, Jean — *Translating Ishi's Stories.* Presentation during "Ishi: The Man and His Times, Revisited" symposium at James More Theater Lecture Hall, The Oakland Museum, CA, March 26, 1994.

Potts, Marie — *The Northern Maidu.* Naturegraph Publishers, Happy Camp, CA, 1977.

Rademacher, Kurt —Presentation on Ishi at Bell Memorial Union, California State University, Chico, Oct. 8, 1991.

— *Saxton Pope's Reminiscences of Ishi.* Presentation during "Ishi: The Man and His Times, Revisited" symposium at James More Theater Lecture Hall, The Oakland Museum, CA, March 26, 1994.

— Also, personal communication.

Ramsey, Tom E. — *East Tehama Deer Herd Plan*. California Department of Fish and Game, Sacramento, 1983.

Rawls, James J. — *Indians of California: The Changing Image*. University of Oklahoma Press, Norman, 1984.

Redden, James E. (editor) — *Papers from the 1987 Hokan — Penutian Languages Workshop*. Department of Linguistics, Southern Illinois University, Carbondale. 1988. Includes presentations by Victor Golla, Leanne Hinton and Herbert W. Luthin.

Riffe, Jed and Roberts, Pamela — *Ishi: The last Yahi* — Jed Riffe Flims, Berkeley. CA, 1992.

— Also, personal communication.

Ritter, Eric W — *Archaeological Test Excavations at Spider Rockshelter (CA-Teh-1432) Lower Mill Creek Canyon*. Bureau of Land Management, Redding, CA, 1987.

— Also, personal communication.

Sapir, Edward and Spier, Leslie — *Notes on the Culture of the Yana*. Anthropological Records, University of California, Berkeley and Los Angeles, 1943.

Serr, Gene (editor) — *Tales from Ishi Country*. Association for Northern California Historical Research, Chico, CA., 2012.

Schulz, Paul E. — *Indians of Lassen Volcanic National Park and Vicinity*. Loomis Museum Association, Mineral, CA, 1988.

Shover, Michele — *California Standoff: Miners, Indians and Farmers at War, 1850-1865*. Stansbury Publishing, Chico, CA, 2017.

— Also, personal communication.

Smith, Richard F. — *Projectile Point Types of the Tehama-Lassen Complex*. Self-published, Redding, CA, 1984.

— Also, personal communication.

Southern, May — Various writings in the archives of the Shasta Historical Society, Redding, CA.

Speegle, Mel — *A Trip to Ishi's Cave*. Oral history recorded by Dorothy Hill, Jan. 28, 1971. Published in the *Dogtown Territorial Quarterly* Winter Edition, Paradise, CA, 1992.

Starn, Orin — Ishi's Brain: In Search of America's Last "Wild" Indian. W.W. Norton and Company, New York, 2004.

Stoddard, Michael — *Vincent Geiger in California. Wagon Wheels*, Colusi County Historical Society, Volume 17, No. 1, Colusa, CA, 1967.

Strobridge, William F. — *Regulars in the Redwoods: The U.S. Army in Northern California 1852-1861*. Arthur A. Clark Co., Spokane, WA, 1994.

Sundahl, Elaine — *Culture Patterns and Chronology in the Northern Sacramento River Drainage*, Society for California Archaeology Proceedings, 1992.

Swartzlow, Ruby Johnson — *Peter Lassen: His Life and Legacy*. Loomis Museum Association, Mineral, CA, 1964.

Tehama County Genealogical and Historical Society — *Tehama County, 1856-2006: 150 Years of Photos and History*. Paragon Publishing, Red Bluff, CA, 2007.

Waterman, John S. — *Old Timer*, a column originally printed in the *Chico Record* in the 1930s, reprinted in the *Chico Enterprise-Record* in the 1980s.

Waterman, Thomas T. — *The Yana Indians*, University of California Publications in American Archaeology and Ethonlogy, Vol. 13, No. 2. Berkeley. 1918. Reprinted in Ishi the Last Yahi.

Wells, Harry L. and Chambers, W.L. — *History of Butte County*. Francis Valentine & Co., San Francisco, 1882.

Milton Keynes UK
Ingram Content Group UK Ltd.
UKHW010712280324
440307UK00001B/98